it's all writ out for you

THE LIFE AND WORK OF SCOTTIE WILSON

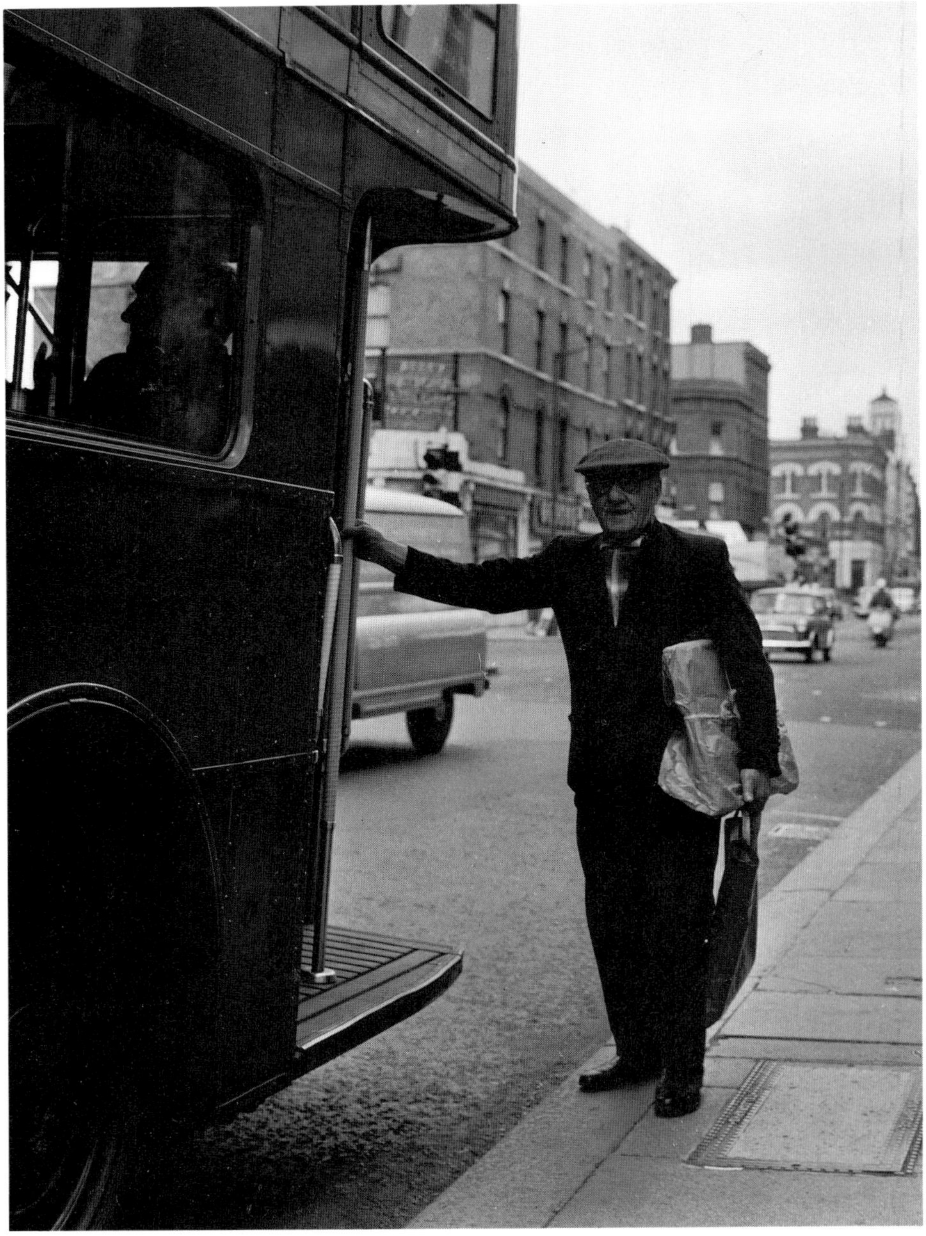

GEORGE MELLY

it's all writ out for you

THE LIFE AND WORK OF SCOTTIE WILSON

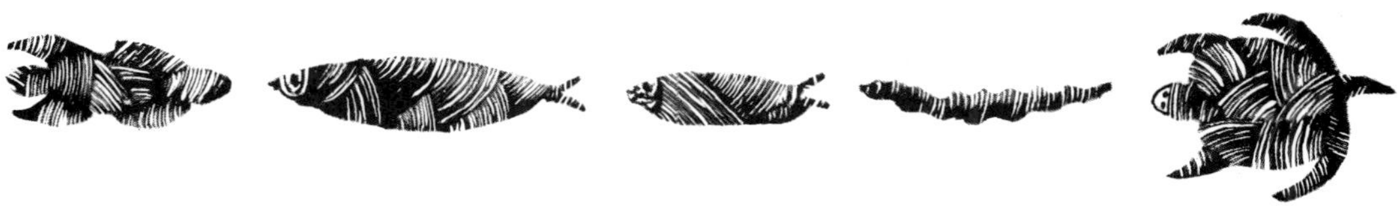

THAMES AND HUDSON

In memory of Victor Musgrave

Note on the plates

The colour pictures are numbered 1–48 and are referred to in the text as 'plates'. Dimensions are given in centimetres, height preceding width. The dates of Scottie's pictures are in almost every case approximate, but the plates have, with the exception of the last, been arranged in chronological groups as far as this is possible to ascertain.

Frontispiece: Scottie in Kilburn, *c.* 1965. Photo: Ida Kar

Printed and bound in Japan by Dai Nippon

CONTENTS

INTRODUCTION

This book is written as a homage to my friend Victor Musgrave whose early death from cancer deprived not only those of us who loved him of a rare and original spirit, but also removed from the art world a man whose insistence on poetry and spontaneity was in so marked a contrast to all those who think of painting and sculpture as a fashionable commodity, a form of visual stocks and shares.

Hearing that he was ill, but unaware how ill, I went to visit him in one of those multi-storeyed new hospitals that resemble a modern hotel. I was shocked by his frail, almost transparent appearance, but touched by his courage and humour, his luminous and undiminished intelligence. I was also amused to find that his manipulative abilities – never directed to his own advantage, always to furthering and promoting what he believed in – were in no way impaired.

In the course of conversation, he let drop in that inimitable, softly discreet voice, that he had been commissioned to write a book on Scottie Wilson, an artist he knew I cherished and whom I had naturally included in my recent book on great British naive painters. It was possible, he said, that he might need some help to finish it. Would I be willing to collaborate? Naturally I said yes. In the event of his remission being shorter than the time it took to complete the book would I perhaps? . . . of course. We spoke of other things. Soon he was clearly tiring, and I left him, promising to return. When I got back off tour he was dead. Entirely selflessly, and only because his enthusiasm for Scottie demanded that he be honoured at greater length and between more substantial covers than had yet been the case, he had landed me with a daunting but unavoidable task. Furthermore I discovered, not without a wry smile, that he had written only a few pages and that all I had to work with were these and a series of note-books, letters, thoughts and comments on little sheets of multi-coloured paper, articles by himself and others on various aspects of Scottie, and two short monographs, one which I already knew and admired, by Mervyn Levy, the other by Gérard A. Schreiner. Nevertheless there was no way that I could or would evade my commitment. In one sense the embryonic state of the material made my task easier. If

Victor had almost completed the book, I would have been forced to assume the role of a pasticheur. As it is I can start from scratch. On the other hand Victor's thoughts about the artist, his descriptions of conversations with Scottie and the documentary material he had collected were a great help. Reading them with attention has forced me to revise my comparative dogmatism about the artist's work and life. Several of my more simplistic ideas have been modified or changed entirely. I have always loved Scottie ever since I first came across his work in the late Forties, but being forced to consider him in depth and in detail has increased my understanding and admiration of his unique contribution to the art of our time. I can only hope that I prove worthy of Victor's trust in me.

I wish to thank in particular Victor Musgrave's *compagnon*, Monika Kinley, who did almost all the research and whose encouragement has been a constant pleasure. I would also like to thank Bob Lewin, Bill Hopkins, Mervyn Levy, Eric Lister, Dr Clifford Myerson, Gimpel Fils, the Fieldbourne Galleries and the Mayor Gallery for the help they gave me in writing and researching this book. The list of exhibitions and bibliography were compiled by Richard Chapman and Mark Gisbourne. I should point out that all the chapter titles, except the first, are remarks by Scottie.

G.M.

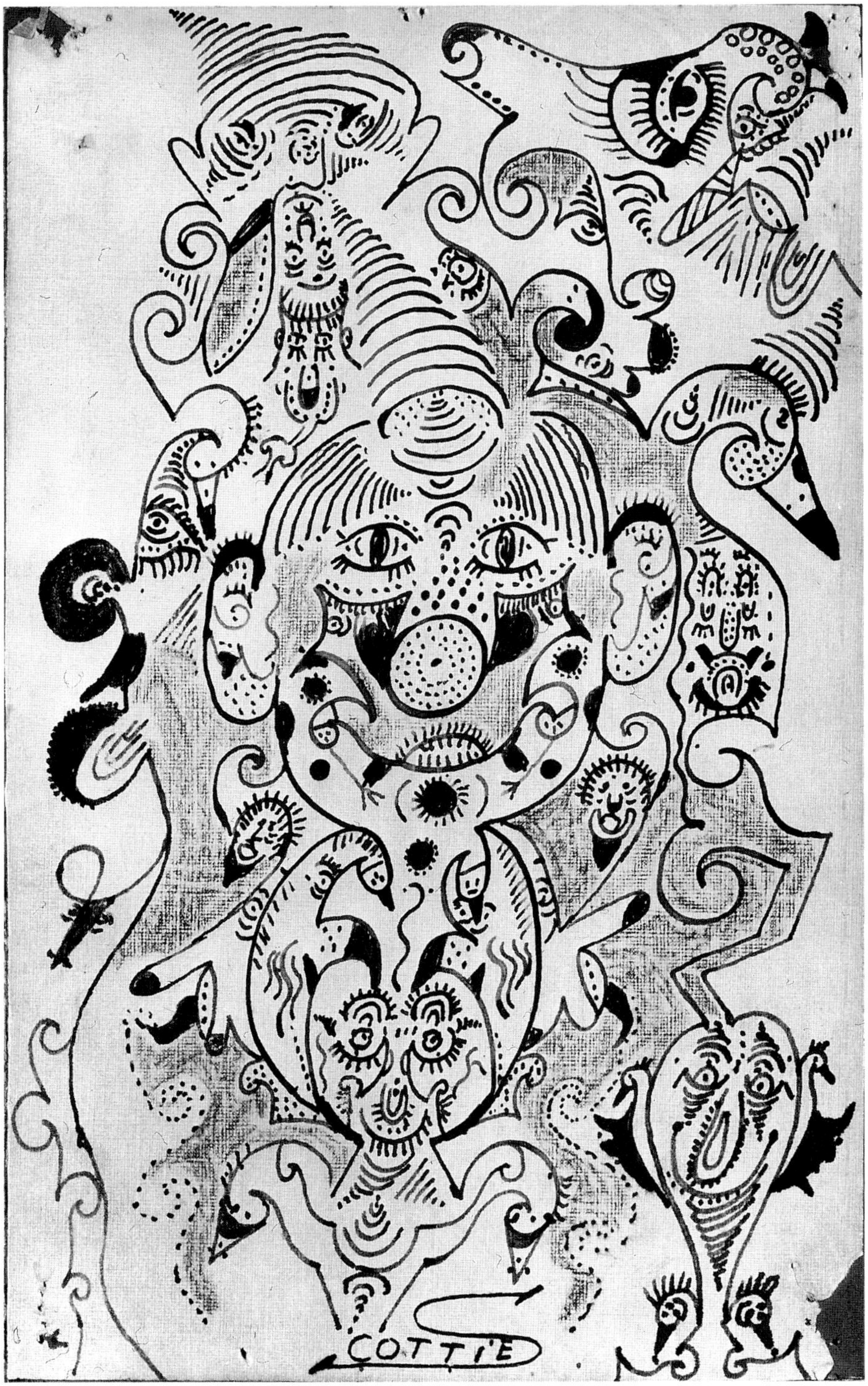

Untitled, *c.* 1930. 20.3×12.7. George Melly

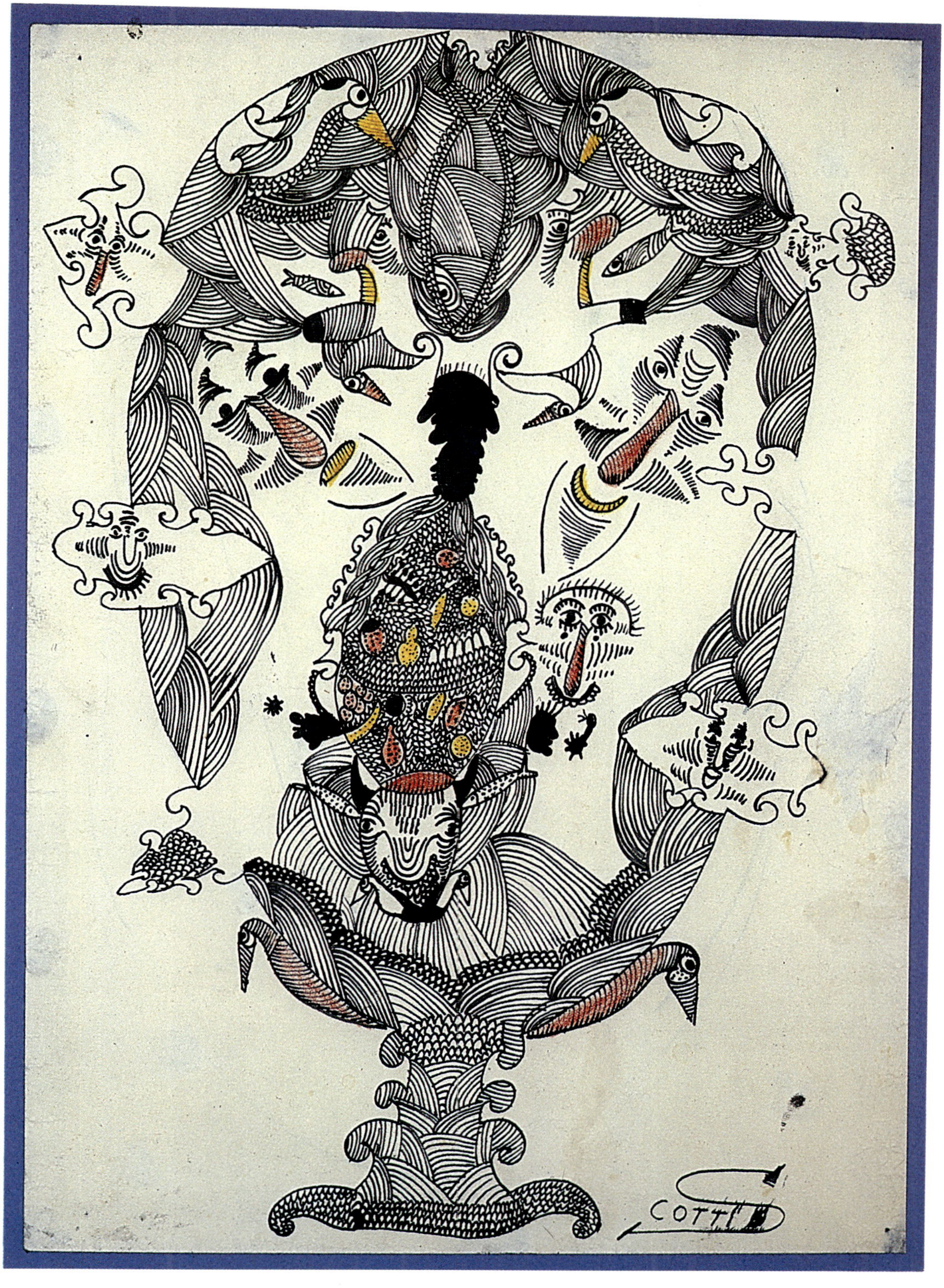

1 Untitled, *c.* 1930. 29.8×21.0. Robert Lewin

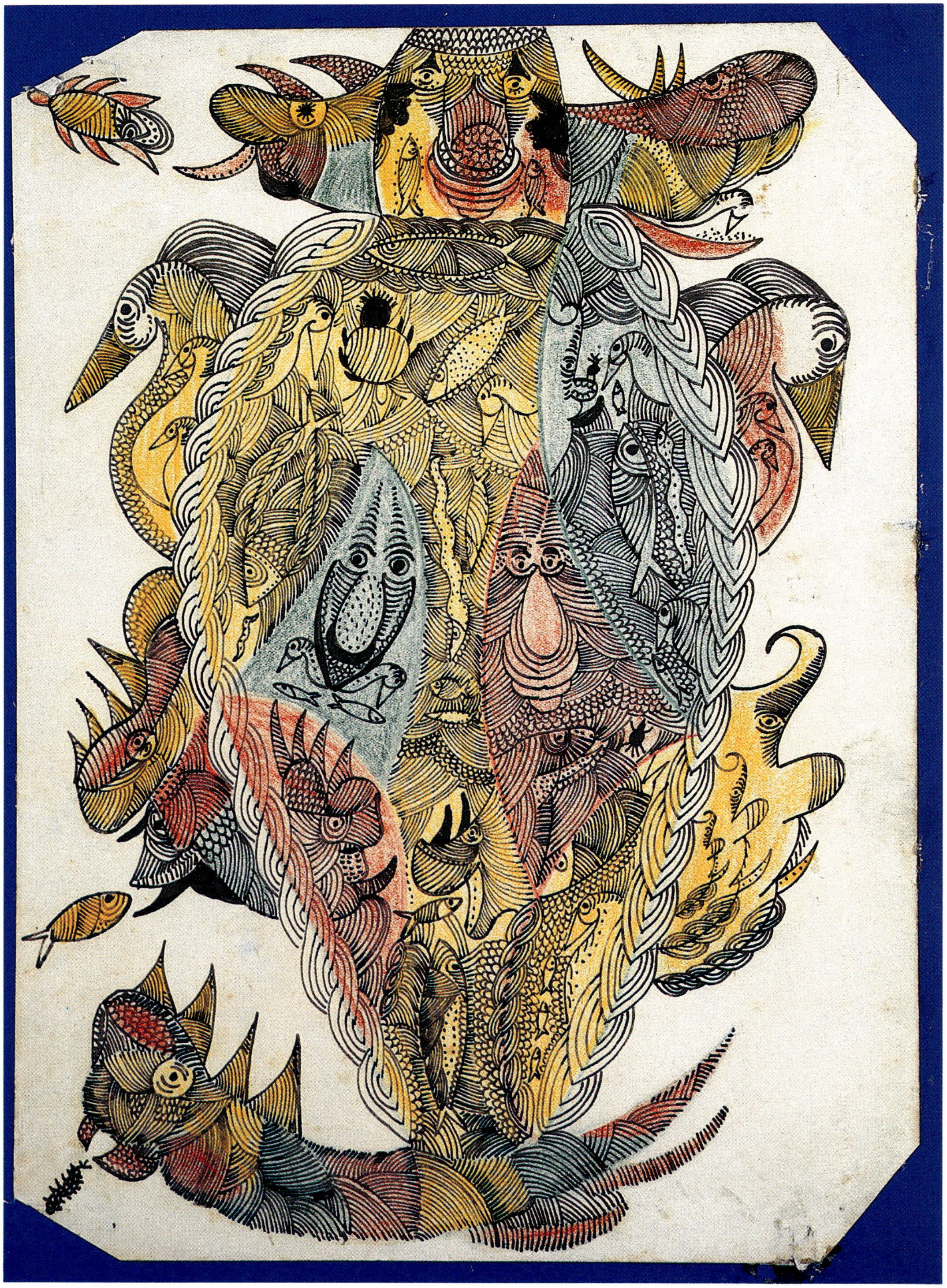

2 *Dream*, *c.* 1930. 30.5×23.0. Gimpel Fils Gallery, London

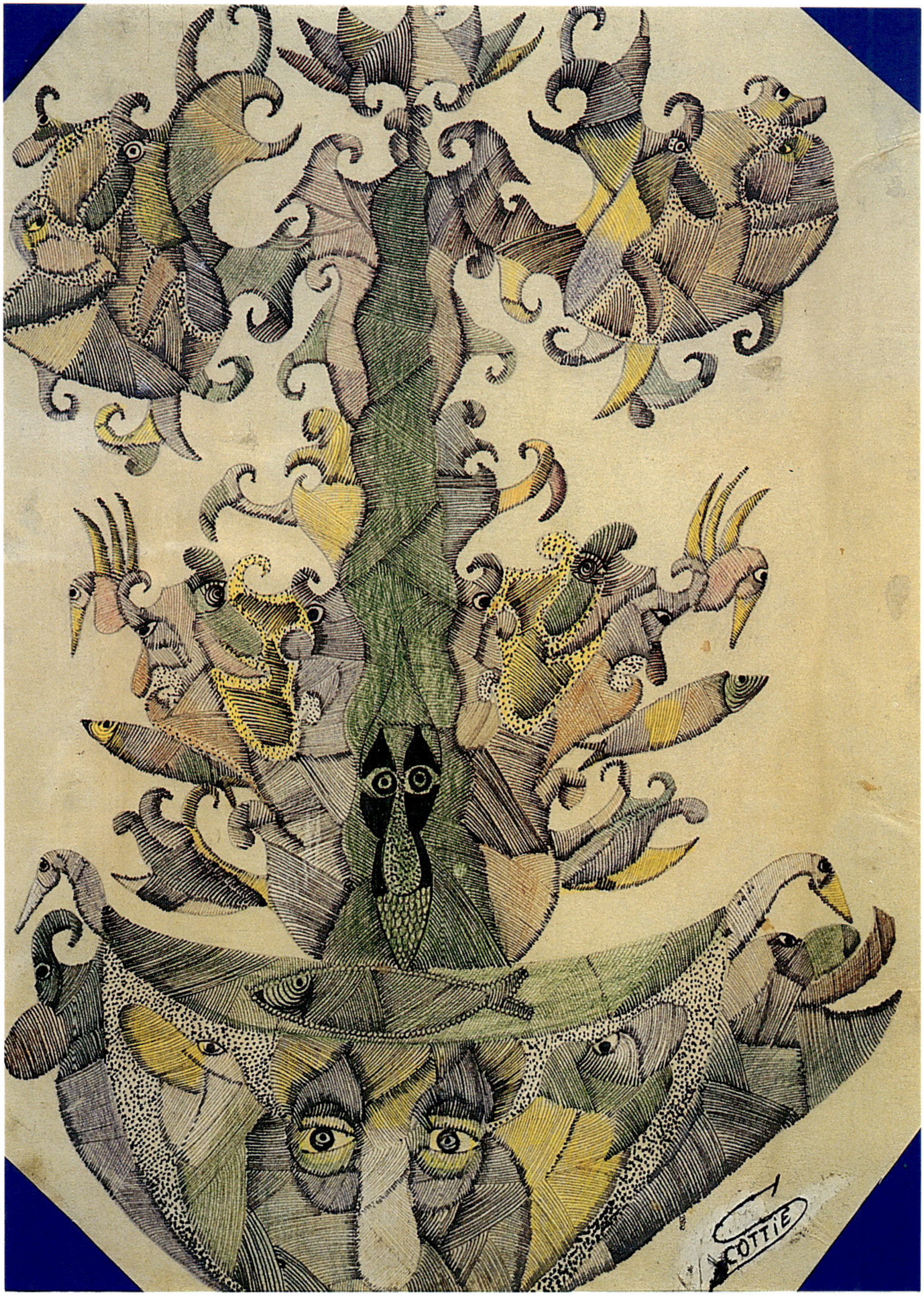

3 Untitled, *c.* 1930. 37.3×27.0. Private collection

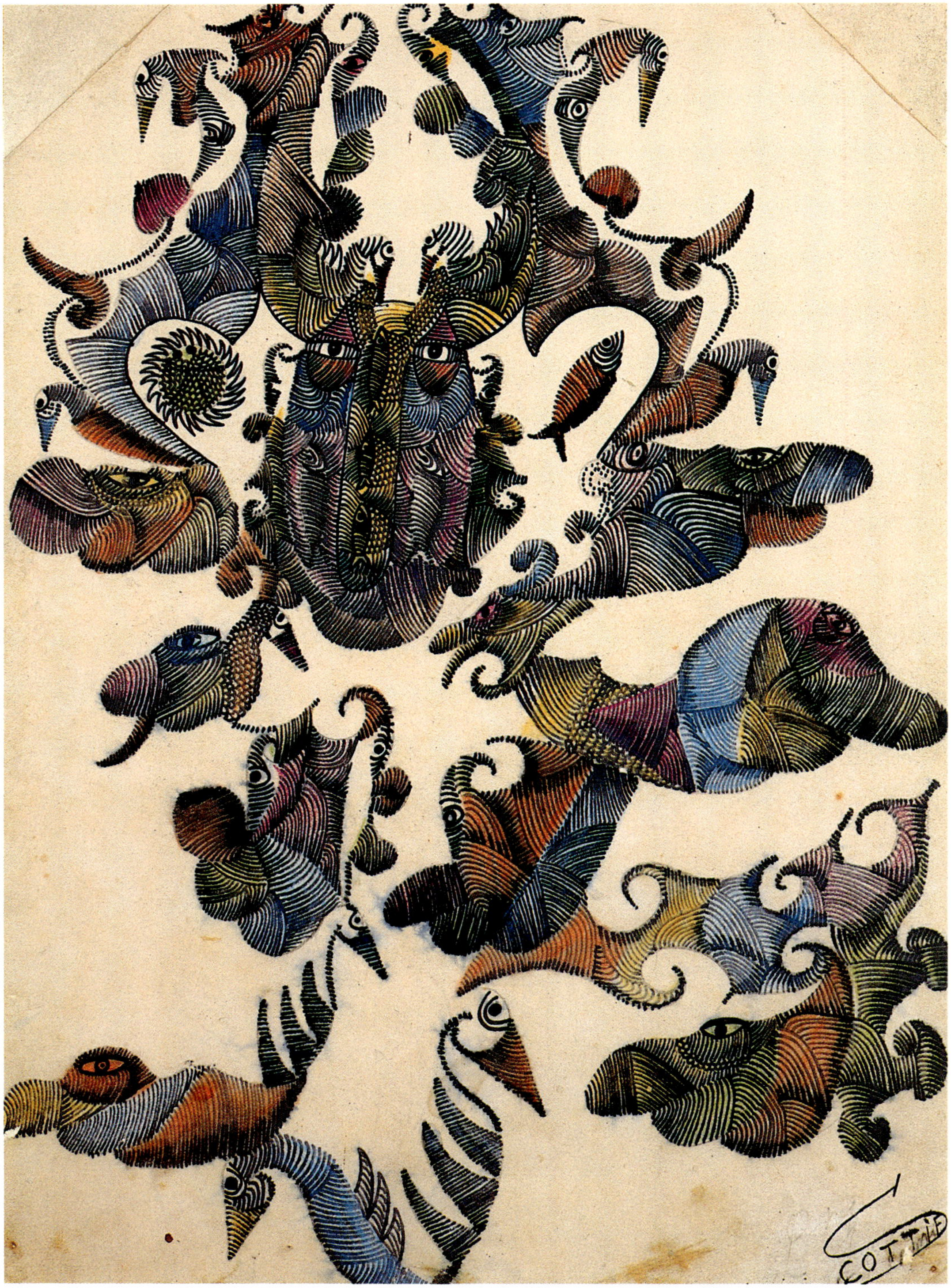

4 *Greedies I*, *c.* 1930. 29.0×21.0. Gimpel Fils Gallery, London

I

Scottie before Scottie

First there was a pen, a pen which Scottie later described as looking 'like a bulldog, with a nib as thick as my finger'. It rested on a card-table given him by a friend because in the back of Scottie's small shop in Toronto there was nowhere to put his radio set. The baize on the card-table had long worn out. It had been replaced by a piece of cardboard. The radio was on the table, playing some Mendelssohn in a concert sponsored by a beer company. Scottie 'all of a sudden', picked up 'the bulldog', dipped it in ink and began to draw on the cardboard. The pen, like the red shoes in Andersen's story, refused to stop. 'Almost continuously . . . the images, the faces and designs just flowed out' said Scottie, as Mervyn Levy recorded in his book on the artist. When the table-top was completely covered Scottie went to Woolworth's, where he bought drawing paper and children's crayons. From then on there was nothing he wanted to do, nothing he could do, but draw.

The exact details of this event vary; it is evident that Scottie added, or embellished, or occasionally forgot some aspect of his moment of revelation or possession although the broad outline remained consistent. In describing it to Mervyn Levy for example, he claimed to have bought the table. To Victor Musgrave on the other hand, Scottie recalled a 'humpty-backed man', with whom he had business dealings who, seeing the radio on the floor, offered him the table to stand it on. Musgrave also reports that it took two weeks to cover the table-top with drawings. E.L.T. Mesens, whom I believe to have written the first article on Scottie published in England (*Horizon*, June 1946), gives no precise moment of creative inspiration, no 'bulldog', no Mendelssohn. In his account, Scottie, faced by financial failure, 'retired more and more frequently into his back shop, where he passed long hours in covering a large piece of beaverboard on his worktable-top with tiny pen strokes'. Levy offers neither 'two weeks' nor 'long hours' for the completion of the first 'Scottie', but two days. At all events, whichever of these details are accurate, all agree on the essentials: at some point between the late Twenties and early Thirties in the back room of a Toronto junk shop, a Glaswegian Jewish second-hand dealer in his early forties, almost illiterate, totally uneducated in the conventional sense, picked up a fountain pen and entered his magic domain.

'Life! – it's all writ out for you – the moves you make.' This was Scottie's most frequently repeated aphorism, not in itself strikingly original, but in his case apposite enough. Suppose for example he had not decided in Toronto to buy up all the fountain pens he could find so as to strip the gold nibs to sell to a refinery ('Gold was fifteen shillings an ounce', he told Musgrave – outside his art, he enjoyed exhibiting the small self-congratulatory cunning of the street-trader). Suppose that among the pens he'd bought for this reason there had been no 'bulldog' to catch his fancy, that the 'humpty-backed' man hadn't given him the card-table or that, if he had, it had still retained its baize. What if there had been no ink handy? Would it have made a difference if, instead of Mendelssohn, the radio had been transmitting a talk or dance music? Suppose that, at the moment Scottie was dipping the pen in the ink and was about to draw his first line, someone had entered the shop, a Canadian person from Porlock, to purchase one of the cut-glass scent bottles which were his principle if curious stock-in-trade?

These are not intended as frivolous questions. What I am asking is, if any one of these conditions had been missing, would Scottie Wilson, ex-newspaper boy, street-trader, soldier, deserter, lumberjack, small-shop-keeper, have then or later or never become an artist? It was not after all a conscious decision. It had never occurred to him that that was what he would like to be. Every moment of our lives is controlled by what we choose to call chance, but few of us experience quite so traumatic an intervention. No wonder Scottie felt 'it's all writ out for you'. Alternatively it seems a clear example of that principle the Surrealists defined as 'the certainty of hazard'.

René Magritte liked to refer to his early Cubist-Futurist works, which preceded his entire change of direction after confronting a reproduction of a De Chirico, as 'Magritte before Magritte'. I feel that at this point (leaving Scottie obsessively covering the surface of the card-table in Toronto over fifty years ago), it is time to describe what little we know (and of that practically none is authenticated) about 'Scottie before Scottie'. The difficulty is that, while the main outlines remain fixed, Scottie frequently varied the details, or would sometimes agree with propositions put forward by his sophisticated interviewers, presumably with an aim to please. This is not uncommon among primitives or innocents, nor is the invention of picturesque adventures.

Researchers into early jazz history frequently run up against the same problem, but it seems to be particularly prevalent amongst those whom I shall categorize for the moment as primitive painters. Henri Rousseau for instance may never have fought in Mexico, and his beasts and tropical vegetation derived from no further afield than the Parisian Jardin des Plantes. There is some doubt as to whether Alfred Wallis, the Cornish naive, ever went to sea, and it is most unlikely that he travelled as far as Labrador as he claimed, despite several very beautiful pictures purporting to represent such a 'voyage'.

It's not exactly deliberate lying in most cases, more a confusion between inner and outer life. The inner life of visionaries is after all more intense than their experience of the mundane world. They achieve, without conscious effort, one of the primary aims of Surrealism: the dismantling of the barrier between dream and reality. In Scottie's case however there is also a suspicion that he enjoyed teasing his inquisitors. While fond of several of them individually, he had a keen mistrust of intellectuals. He tended, when exasperated, to call them 'mouthpieces'.

It never occurred to me, when I first met Scottie in the late Forties, that he was anything other than Scottish. Quite apart from his thick Glaswegian brogue, his whole appearance – mended spectacles, grog-blossom nose, canny expression, cloth cap, muffler, long overcoat, boots, and an habitual Woodbine between his fingers – suggested either a music-hall comedian in the tradition of Will Fyffe or one of those near-vagrants who approach one in the streets surrounding the north London rail termini and aggressively demand small change for 'a cuppa tea, Jimmy'. In fact, I was to discover much later, he was not of Scottish descent at all, but Jewish, something he never mentioned at that time, or at any rate not to me. He did however once describe to a friend, George Murray, a very unpleasant anti-semitic incident in a Canadian bar. He spoke of it as if it involved a third person. Couldn't it have been he who was the victim of it? Certainly Murray reports that later on, when he tried to show Scottie a book on Jewish artists, 'Scottie appeared upset and didn't want to know'. Was it possibly anti-semitism in general or that specific incident in the Canadian bar which decided Scottie, born Louis Freeman, to change his name to Wilson? It's true that, late in life, he exhibited at the Ben Uri, a gallery devoted to Jewish artists, but the catalogue makes no reference to Scottie's Jewish origins. I myself suspect that the suppression of this, his exaggerated Glaswegian persona, is somehow psychologically important to both his life and work. The poet and playwright Bill Hopkins, another friend of Scottie's, told me however that once in the Fifties Scottie spoke of the greatness of Heine, and went on further to enthuse about the brilliance of the Jewish race. Hopkins was surprised, not only that the illiterate painter had ever heard of Heine, but also that as a working-class Glaswegian, in general anti-semitic by definition, he should praise the Jewish race. Scottie didn't however reveal or even hint that he himself was Jewish.

On the other hand, to Clifford Myerson, his doctor and close friend during his later years, and as his name suggests a fellow Jew, there was no concealment. Not only that but Scottie, despite his generally anarchistic philosophy and his belief that greed and power were the causes of all the evils of the world, revealed himself as a passionate Zionist and an entirely uncritical admirer of Golda Meir. He took it for granted, and incorrectly says Dr Myerson, 'that I was an equally committed Zionist. I saw no point in correcting him. It would only have upset him.' Dr Myerson confirms Scottie's obsession with anti-semitism, a word, which like so many others, he pronounced incorrectly.

Scottie was born on 6 June 1888. His parents, according to a letter Victor Musgrave received in 1984 from one of Scottie's nephews, Alan Freeman, had emigrated from Lithuania in the second half of the 19th century. They landed in Hull, where the immigration clerk, unable or unwilling to write down their complicated Russian-sounding name, rebaptized them Freeman. They settled in Glasgow, where Mr Freeman eventually found work as a taxidermist's assistant. To Dr Myerson, however, Scottie maintained that his father was a furrier, although this doesn't necessarily rule out the possibility that he pursued both professions simultaneously or changed from one to the other at a later date. Scottie also told his doctor that he was born not in Glasgow but in the East End of London, and that they did not move to Scotland until he was three or four.

The Freemans had three sons, Philip, Jack and Louis (Scottie). It is typical of Scottie's tendency to fantasize that he should later speak of 'four brothers of whom three were "bad", and only one of whom he recalled with affection', as Roger Cardinal records in *Outsider Art*. Scottie left school early, at the age of nine, and still, as he was to remain, more or less illiterate. To help his family, he worked as 'a barefoot newspaper boy', not in those days an uncommon sight. I myself can remember bare-footed children in the streets of Liverpool as late as the 1930s. Victor Musgrave, in the notes he prepared for this book, points out that, perhaps in consequence, boots for Scottie became an obsession in later life. In comparative prosperity he bought them from an expensive bootmaker in St James's and they were always highly polished and in marked contrast to the rest of his rather 'down on his luck' appearance. Mervyn Levy notes that they were not even ordinary boots. He bought riding boots, had them cut down and eased them on with talcum powder.

From selling newspapers he gravitated to market-trading, initially by helping the vendors to set up their stalls and push their barrows. One of his brothers, Joseph according to Scottie (but Jack could have been his nickname), was himself a street trader who sold a herbal mixture which was alleged to make you strong. The highpoint of his spiel came when young Scottie, standing beside him, 'tore off his shirt and flexed his muscles to demonstrate the effectiveness of this nostrum' (Musgrave's notes). Later in life Scottie would occasionally go to a post office and send this brother a postal order for five pounds.

Life was hard for Scottie during his Glaswegian childhood, but he was to recall certain moments of intense illumination. He often spoke of a large fountain in a public park that impressed him. It was carved from that pinkish brown stone typical of so many of the buildings and monuments of the city. He was also very drawn towards the circus and the zoo, having particular fondness for the elephant. He spoke affectionately to Musgrave of 'a seal, a dog, a cat and a little budgie'. He would, he added, frequently feed the birds in the backyard. Another contact with creatures, albeit dead ones, was through his father's work as a taxidermist: fish or game preserved for Scottish sportsmen, other animals destined for museums. As a child Scottie loved chocolates and boiled sweets, a taste he retained all his life. He would usually have some about his person and would offer them freely, sometimes to the surprise of visitors to his exhibitions in West End galleries.

In 1906, when he was eighteen, he joined the Scottish Rifles, serving first in India and then South Africa. At Bloemfontein in 1911 he bought himself out. Mervyn Levy has written down Scottie's account of this incident:

> Having just made a substantial 'killing' on the Crown and Anchor board [a dicing game], he was sweltering along the dusty south African roads with a column of Infantry, his clothes and pockets loaded with coins and a heavy money belt rubbing painfully against his flesh, when he suddenly realised that he was now in

a position to buy himself out of the army. He gradually fell behind, watched the tail of the column disappear over a hill and trudged back to base where he at once paid for his discharge. But the balance of his money was soon exhausted and he worked his passage back to England as a ship's stoker.

There is a charmingly Chaplinesque feel to this tale, but I have some doubts as to its factual accuracy. To desert a marching column and buy oneself out, as casually as if making a purchase in a shop, seems unlikely. Surely a bureaucracy like the army would insist on a more formal approach?

In 1914 Scottie rejoined the Scottish Rifles, and saw service on the Western front. After his demobilization he returned to street trading, first in Glasgow, then in London, where he graduated from a stall in the Caledonian Road to a small shop in the Edgware Road, a district which clearly suited him as in later life it was there he occupied a series of small rented rooms. After some years he left England for Canada. Or so goes the received story, but Alan Freeman, son of Scottie's brother Philip and now an Israeli citizen, proposed, in the letter to Victor Musgrave mentioned above, a much more dramatic twist to the story, and an alternative reason for his change of name. 'You wrote in your article: he left England for Canada. Actually he left Ireland for Canada, which is also the reason why he changed his name to Robert Wilson (Scottie was of course because of his Glasgow Gorbals accent). In Martin Rayner's article, he states that my Uncle was sent to Ireland with the Black and Tans and, according to my Father, his conscience wouldn't allow him to carry out the Army orders and he deserted and went to Canada.'

Dr Clifford Myerson has a variant on this story which Scottie himself told him. In this version Scottie was in France and advancing with his platoon through a wood where there was a fork and the order was to take the left-hand path. Those ahead of him who did so were mowed down so Scottie quite deliberately turned to the right and eventually found himself at a Red Cross Unit where, for three days, he helped carry in the wounded. Once when he was sleeping, a Colonel arrived, saw him and asked who he was and what he was doing there. It might have gone badly for him if it hadn't been for the surgeon in charge who praised his courage under fire, and no further enquiries were made. 'There's a bit of a gap there,' says Dr Myerson, 'but he told me that he did desert to Ireland and hid in a house there which also was harbouring several I.R.A men who impressed Scottie deeply. He then somehow escaped to Canada.'

Either version explains the change of name rather neatly, but Scottie himself always stuck to the more prosaic return to street trading and the shop in the Edgware Road, after his war service. It could be however that he did so out of caution, uncertain whether the Army might still harbour an unwelcome interest in him even after so long a period of time. Either way it is certain that he went to Canada. After a time he came back to England but then, for whatever reason, felt compelled to return again to Canada where he moved around from city to city selling here tinned meat and jam, there second-hand furniture. Eventually he settled in Toronto, with his stock of scent bottles and bundles of old fountain pens. It is there we left him, and there we rejoin him raptly at work on the cardboard surface of the card-table.

2

'It's there – it's always been there – it's you'

With his obsessive devotion to drawing established, Scottie began to spend all his time in the backroom of his shop and in consequence his business, never I imagine much of a money-spinner, declined to near zero. He covered the walls with his pictures – 'saved buying wallpaper' – and exhibited some in his window. It was not long before they attracted the admiring attention of several dealers and academics. A Mr Douglas Duncan was the first, according to Scottie, to show sustained enthusiasm for his work. Professor Norman Endicott of the University of Toronto was also an early admirer. Both began to buy Scotties; and this was very necessary for his survival as the scent bottles and gold-tipped fountain pens – with the exception of the 'bulldog' – were no longer of much concern or profit to him.

Nevertheless his success must have produced some contradictory feelings in Scottie Wilson in that both then and later he disliked having to sell any of his pictures – a quite common trait among self-taught visionaries – although he felt less reluctant to give them away to those who really appreciated them. His solution, until well into later life, was to alleviate his dismay at being forced to live off his works by exhibiting them, for viewing only, in tents, empty shops, disused cinema foyers and even, on one occasion, a hired bus, charging admission and making a silver collection. He could however at times, even in these situations, occasionally be persuaded to sell them, usually for a fraction of the sum demanded by those dealers who stocked his work, a practice which caused these gentlemen considerable frustration and irritation. Scottie held a high opinion of his own pictures. He once claimed that if he were rich he would buy them all himself.

The early Canadian pictures, sometimes with, sometimes without colour, lack, initially at any rate, the assurance, the confident structure, of his work in the later Thirties and throughout the Forties. They are closer to doodling, and closer also to the work of schizophrenics and other alienated souls. Nevertheless the impact is entirely convincing, as complex, if less seductive, as his later developments. The close-knitting of his penstrokes is still to come. There are cone-like, diminishing lines and

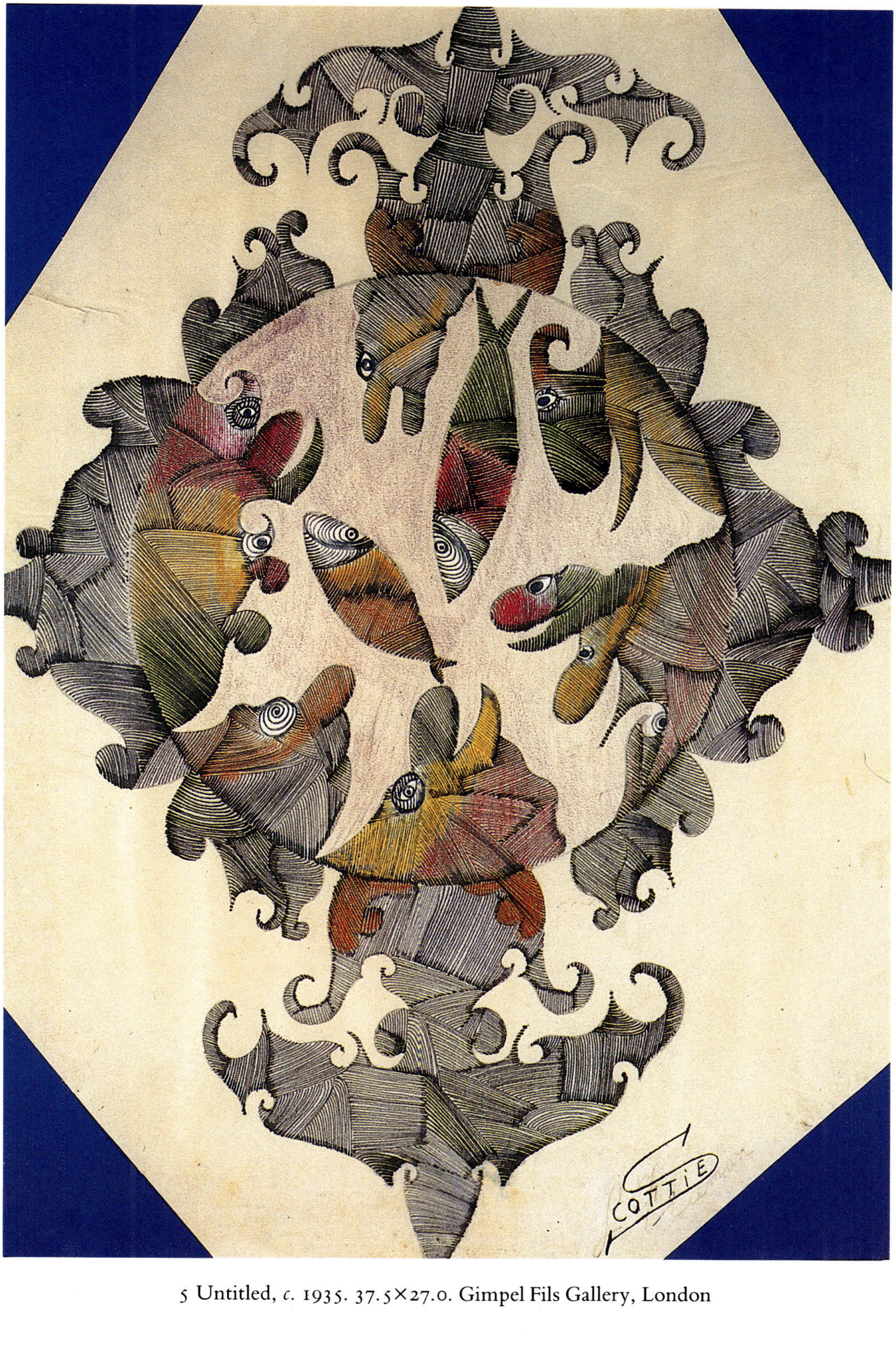

5 Untitled, *c.* 1935. 37.5×27.0. Gimpel Fils Gallery, London

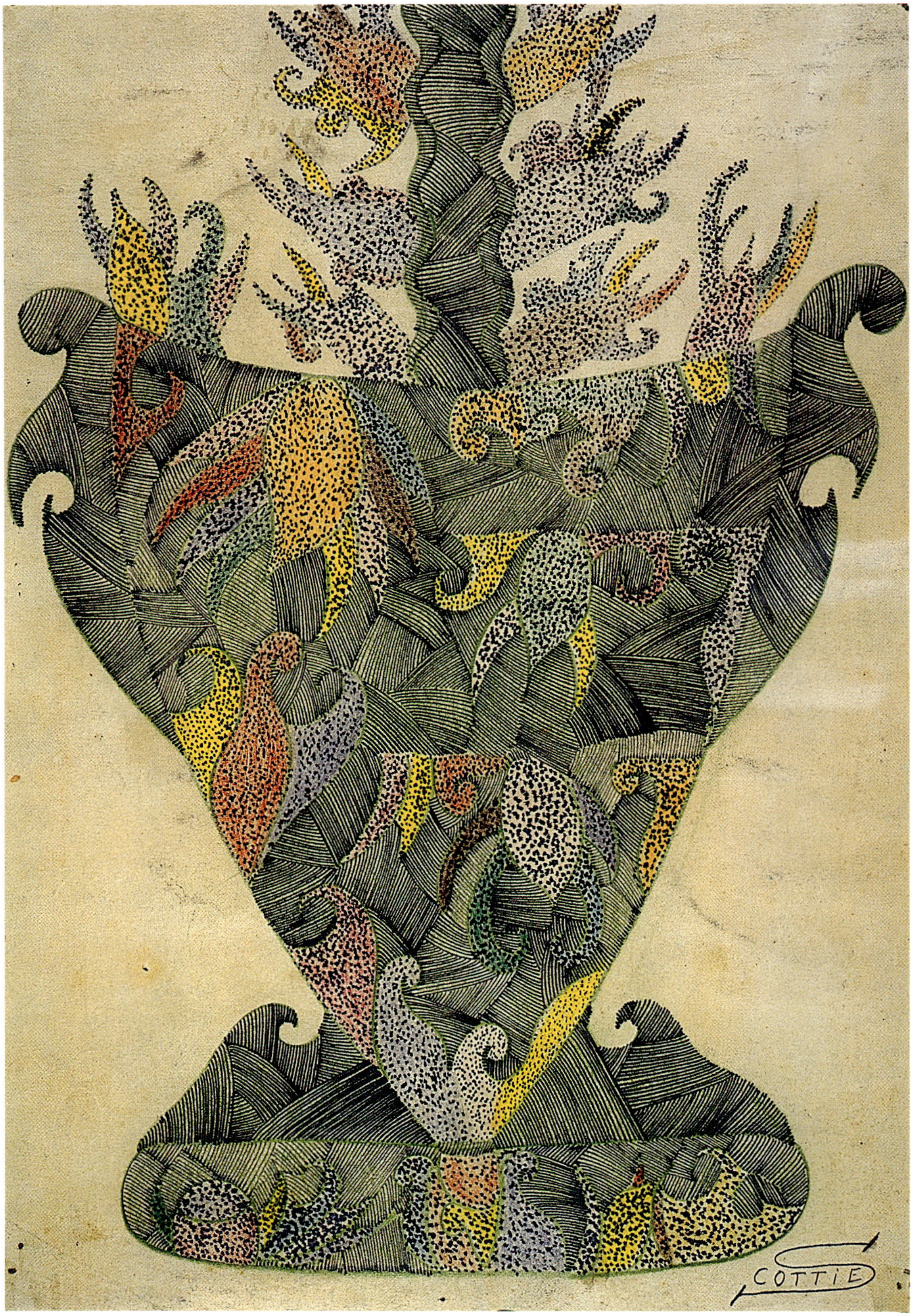

6 Untitled, *c.* 1935. 37.0×26.3. Private collection

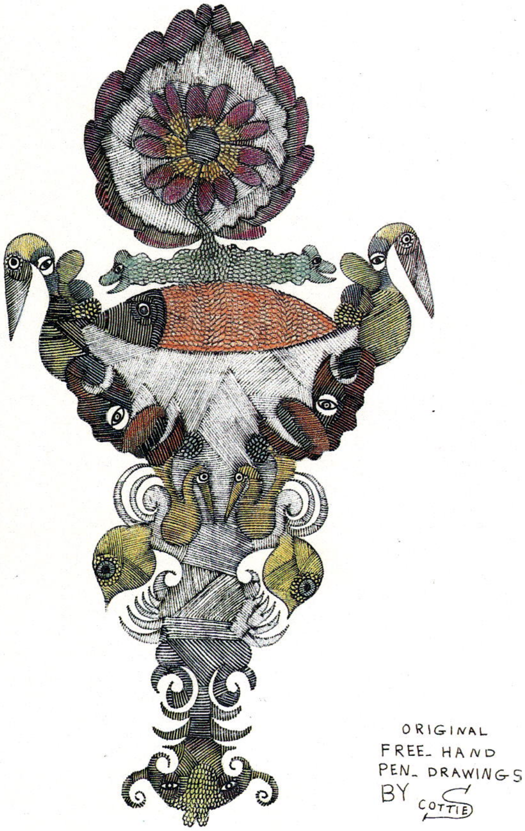

7 Untitled, *c.* 1935. 38.1×27.9.
Mayor Gallery, ex Roland Penrose collection

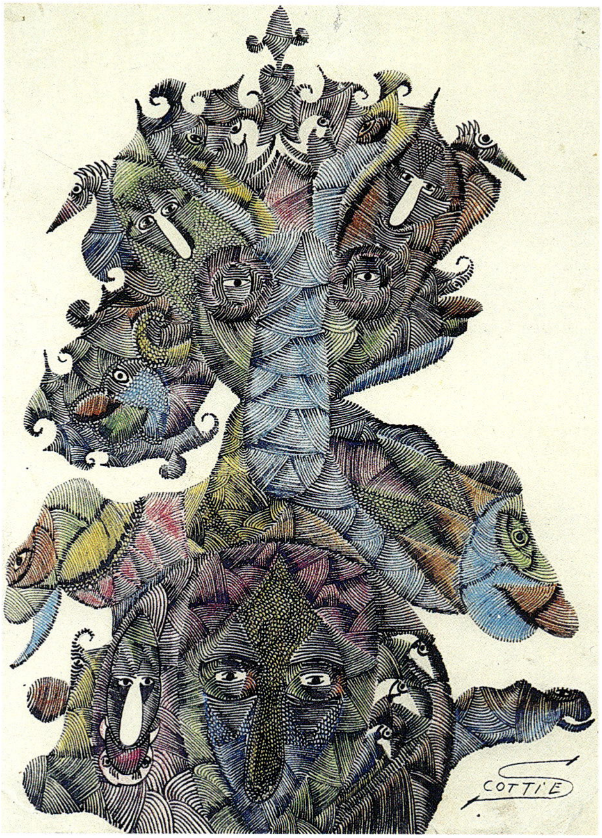

8 Untitled, *c.* 1935. 29.8×22.2.
Robert Lewin

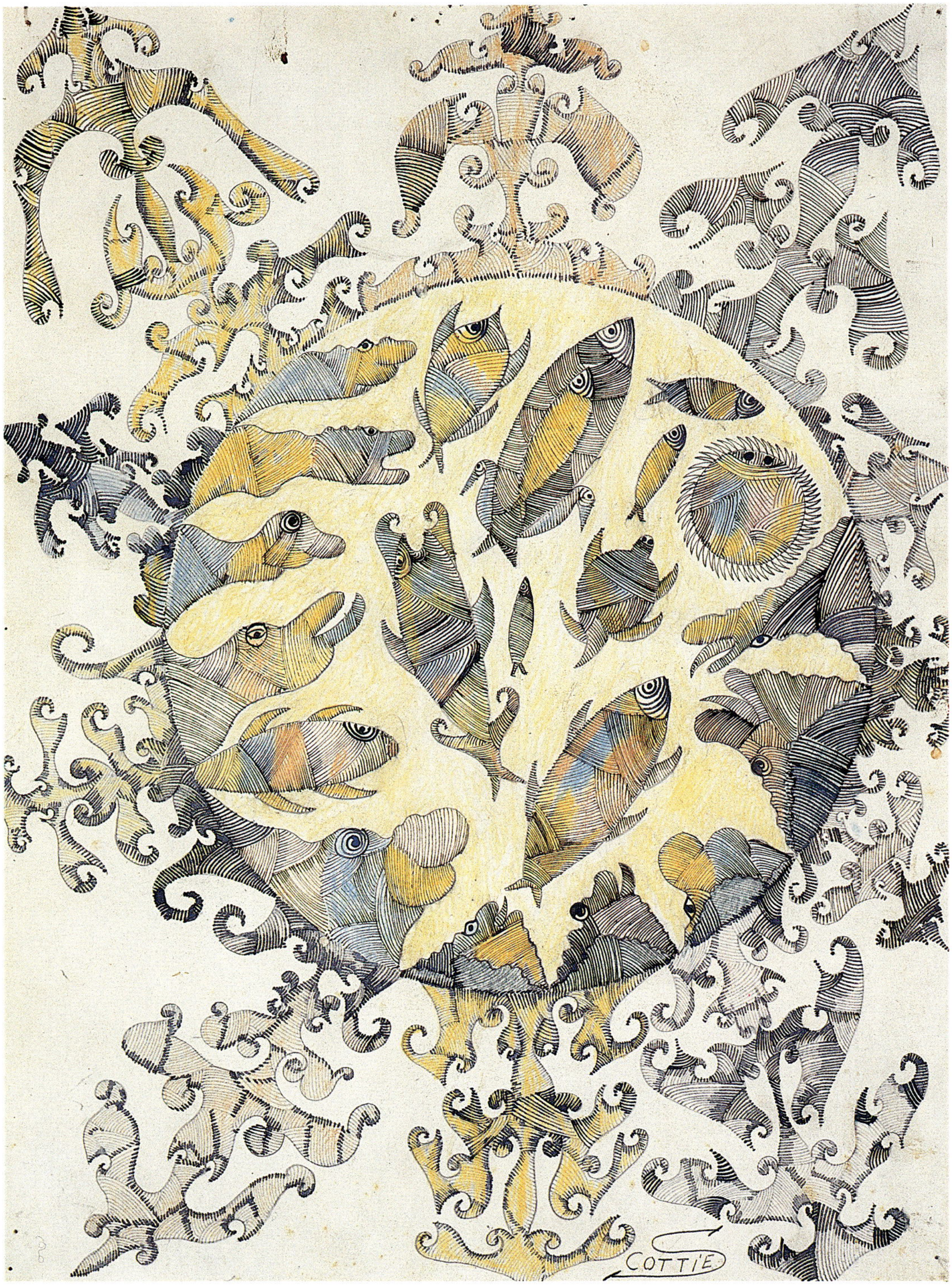

9 Untitled, *c.* 1945. 38.0×28.0. Collection de L'Art Brut, Lausanne

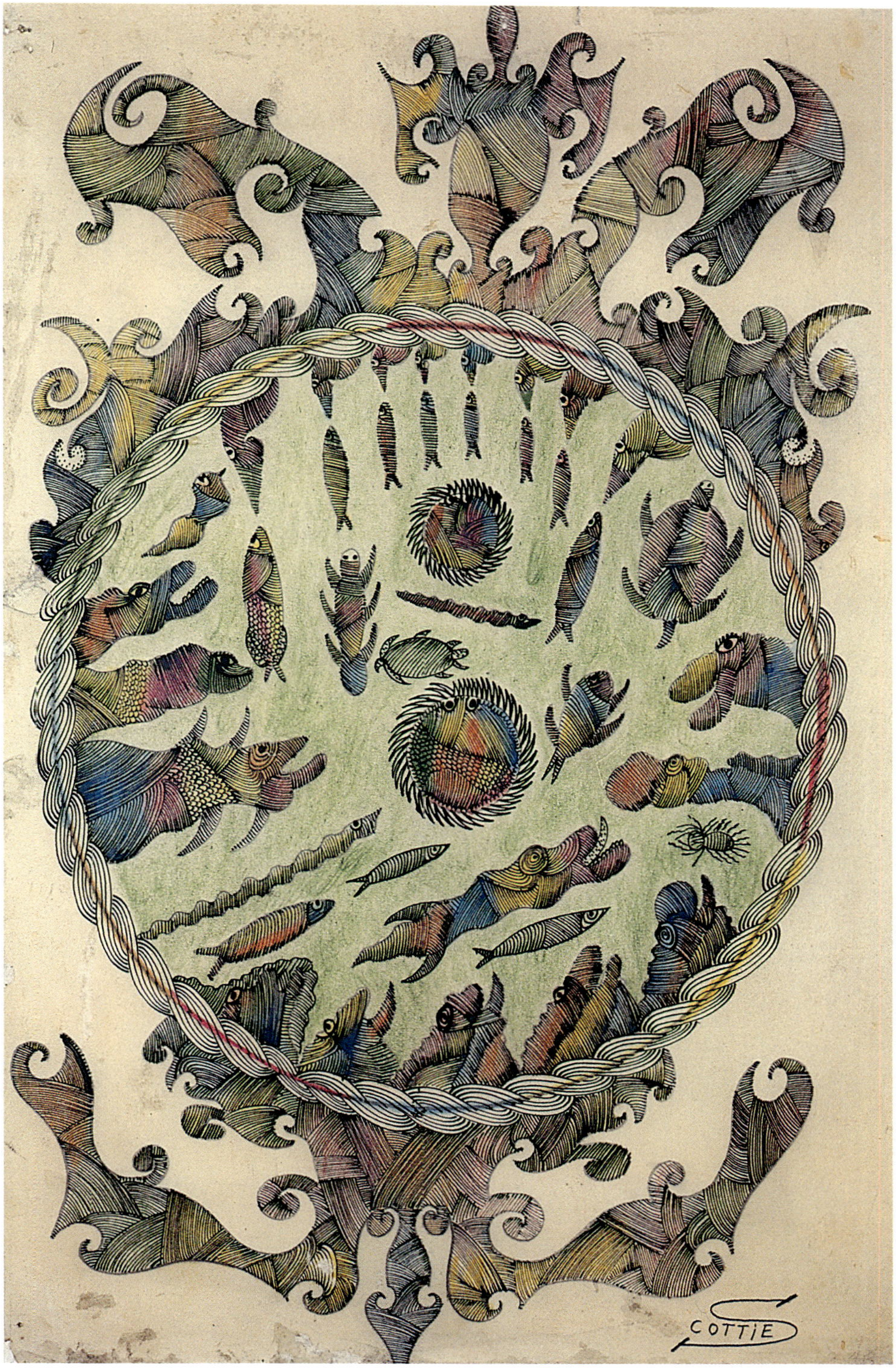

10 Untitled, *c.* 1940. 38.1×25.4. Robert Lewin

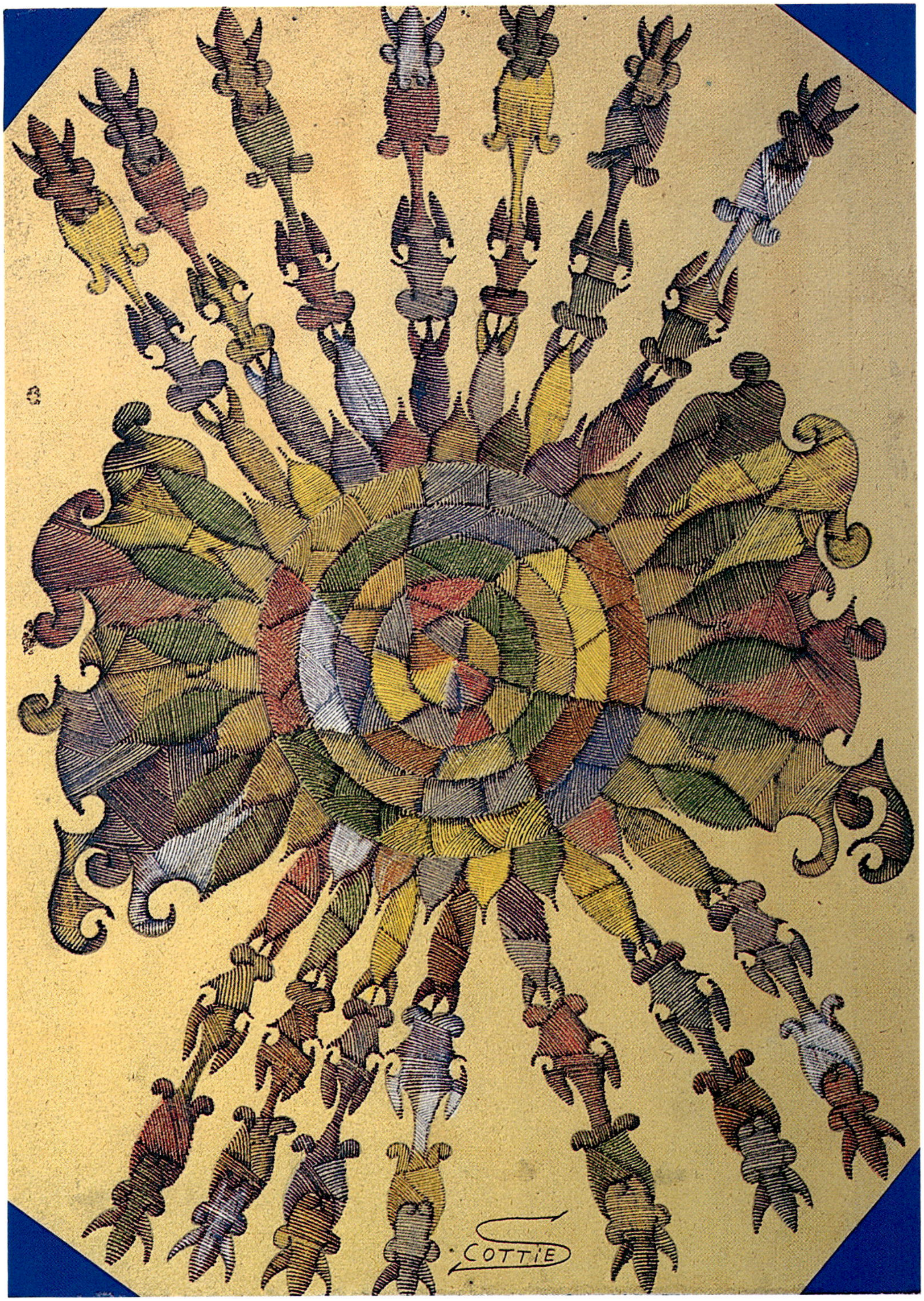

11 Untitled, *c.* 1940. 38.1×26.7. Robert Lewin

systems of dots. Much of the imagery which was to haunt him throughout his creative life is already present: the clown faces (himself), the birds, the fish. The more sinister and menacing creatures he was to call the 'Greedies' or the 'Evils' are still only embryonic little demons, usually in black silhouette, like agitated parasites.

Equally in evidence, on occasion more in evidence, are the phallic and vaginal puns (usually noses and mouths) which were to persist throughout his work. Victor Musgrave especially was to comment on the latent sexual content of Scottie's iconography: the birds with their long beaks penetrating the ears of his personages, the vagina-like mouths overhung by elongated, usually flaccid noses, the limp but extended tongues. Musgrave also cites more generalized phallic imagery – fishes, vases, cupolas, spires, cones, chimneys – and the equivalent female elements of circles, orifices, fishponds, petals, and ovals of all kinds. It is my view that, while sexual elements are clearly present in Scottie's work, it is not exclusively, or even predominantly, a vehicle for sexual sublimation. On the other hand to deny this element would be perverse.

E.L.T. Mesens for instance once proposed to me that what he described in his *Horizon* article as 'those thousands of little strokes patiently aligned', were perhaps a substitute for masturbation, a theory it would have been difficult to expound in a published article in the late Forties, and which anyway would have almost certainly outraged the reticent Scottie, especially if it were an accurate supposition. Musgrave himself tried to interrogate Scottie on the subject of his sex-life but with scant although significant results. 'I knew Scottie intermittently but well over some twenty years and it will be seen that I had formed the opinion than his sex-life remained unfulfilled.' Earlier in the same article he writes: 'I was never able to draw Scottie out on the subject of women. They did not seem to exist in his life.'

The painter Lucian Freud, who knew Scottie well in the early years after his return to England, also tried to 'draw him out on the subject of women'. 'It was very curious', says Freud. 'He would discuss them, but in a distant, almost abstract way, as if he were talking about the solar system.' This would seem to confirm Musgrave, but Dr Myerson gathered a very different impression. Scottie told him that he'd had a lot of trouble from women all his life, and also that he had lived for a time with a woman in King's Cross. After a prostate operation in his late seventies, he asked the doctor if it would affect his sex-life, but Myerson believes that, given his age, he was probably referring to masturbation.

Still, Scottie confided to his doctor much that he concealed from the world at large.

Although he saw Victor Musgrave intermittently over many years, Scottie only once broached the subject of a woman in his life, and that in a somewhat opaque manner from which Musgrave found himself unable to draw a definitive conclusion.

Now, for the first time since I had known him, he mentioned one in what was more than a passing aside on the wife of a friend or a collector. This was a woman whom he said he respected, admired and loved, a clever and perceptive business woman. I could not bring myself to enquire into the relationship, but for some reason I felt it was platonic. When she saw the completed card-table she told Scottie he was a born artist. It sounded so silly to him he thought she had gone crazy. It appeared that this woman, for reasons of her own, then withdrew from whatever involvement she had in his life, saying that he had something to give the world. The event is opaque but the essence of it is there: it resembles what I believe psychiatrists call the Beatrice and Dante syndrome. Scottie, in his own words, was heartbroken. When he spoke of her years later, his voice had a catch in it. He could not forget her . . .

Certainly, the early work which I have seen, while largely self-centred, is without that joy and certainty which, in opposition to the external threat offered by the demonic 'Greedies' and 'Evils', permeates so much of his later production. The raw and undeveloped, but never tentative, technique does nothing to weaken the desperate alienation of the pictures that immediately followed the card-table. Indeed, the later externalization of the 'Greedies' and the 'Evils' was a healthy sign. In the early work it is Scottie's clown-like self portraits (although they were always to remain melancholic) which express unalleviated anxiety and some despair.

In that these early pictures resemble in impact and technique works produced by the insane or mentally disturbed, they can, I suppose, be compared to what Musgrave and Roger Cardinal have termed 'Outsider Art' and Dubuffet 'L'Art Brut', but it is my view that later on, when the optimistic and pessimistic elements are separately defined and set in opposition to each other, and an aesthetic system controls both the use of colour and the asymmetric overall design, this definition is no longer strictly applicable. Nor, on the other hand, was Scottie in the exact sense a naive (although I myself have been guilty of defining him as such). The naive, however inexpertly, looks out at reality and tries, within his powers, to represent it. Scottie never did this. There is no attempt to represent perspective or depth in his work. It was always drawn, in both senses of the word, from what André Breton has called 'the interior model', a concept recognized by Roger Cardinal in his book *Outsider Art*.

Indeed the Surrealists were immediately convinced by Scottie when introduced to his work by E.L.T. Mesens shortly after the war. Gérard A. Schreiner, in a monograph published by his gallery in Basel in 1979, disposes briskly of the attempts to claim Scottie either as an 'outsider' or a 'naive', and places him in 'a direct line of descent from the surrealist attitude, because surrealism was never a means of expression, but rather one of spiritual liberation, a cry of the mind'. True enough, except that the Surrealists were conscious of what they were doing, even when courting, with greater or lesser success, automatic processes. Naturally they admired, even perhaps envied Scottie. Schreiner's own shot at 'placing' Scottie is to describe him as 'an innocent' because, he maintains, 'the innocent see more clearly . . . Their innocence does not spring from a choice, or a philosophical process, but from a real and honest lack of knowledge.' While believing that Scottie Wilson had some characteristics in common with 'outsiders', 'naives' and the Surrealists, I find Schreiner's definition the most relevant. Scottie was, for all his knowing ways, 'an innocent'.

I have seen comparatively little of Scottie's early work, although I own an example, but, around the middle of the Thirties, a great leap forward took place. E.L.T. Mesens, in his *Horizon* article, described it with admirable precision. 'The early works, as far as I can make out – for Scottie has very little sense of data – have very much the aspect of doodlings. But doodlings with a central theme: himself . . . The colouring of these early drawings – already at this time he used crayon – is not very convincing, but altogether they are remarkable documents. After that something must have happened in Scottie's life, because the drawings which follow become suddenly very firm, masterly in writing, and very rich and distinguished in colour . . .'

This is evident to the eye, but what Mesens calls Scottie's 'little sense of data' can create confusion. He never dated, was perhaps unable to date, his work and later on, when a dealer or collector asked him to do so, was extremely, sometimes absurdly, approximate. For instance, there are two pictures reproduced by Mervyn Levy. One he calls *Happy Seascape* (pl. 1), the other *Masquerade*. Scottie in retrospect dated them both as 1940; an impossible supposition as by that time his mature style had fully evolved. *Happy Seascape* is obviously much earlier in its use of broken lines and detached objects. *Masquerade* I suspect is a little later, a transitional work, in that the faces, fish and birds are more or less contained in a large although incomplete vase-shape, and the quilted use of parallel lines, primitive and approximate in *Happy Seascape*, is a bit closer to his fully evolved practice, but even here the diminishing cones and free-floating faces and objects are nearer to the early, unresolved 'doodling' than to the magisterial certainty of his mature work. By the middle Thirties, however, he has entirely resolved his technique. There is still, for a short time, the occasional use of dots instead of lines, but the characteristic 'stitching' and 'fish-scaling' predominates, and the containing shape of each picture, whether formal or organic, is confidently established.

It is not known for sure the year that Scottie covered the card-table; anytime between 1928 and 1931 has been suggested. Nor has it been possible to establish how long the 'doodling' and transitional periods lasted but, as Mesens recognized, there is a certain moment, most likely around 1934–5, when it becomes obvious that he had found his way. Scottie himself was perfectly aware of this development. In an interview in a Vancouver newspaper during an exhibition in the Forties he is quoted as saying 'I've come a long way since my early doodling years ago . . . I've gradually gained more and more feeling for design and now each picture has to be just right before I can call it finished.' In the same article he re-insists on his reluctance to sell his work but admits that Douglas Duncan, his earliest supporter, had persuaded him, in Toronto, to allow him to buy no less than twenty-five for his collection. 'The ones he liked were all my favourites,' said Scottie, 'with the exception of one. I miss them.'

This helps to emphasize still further the gap between Scottie Wilson and the true naive or outsider. However automatic the impulse behind his work, he was able, although perhaps not to begin with, to look at it objectively enough to realize when it was complete and to judge it work by work. For most naives this is not the case. Alfred Wallis for example couldn't understand and was indeed offended by the preference his admirers displayed for one picture over another. James Dixon, the Tory Island fisherman-painter, was equally perplexed when his discoverer and mentor, the artist Derek Hill, showed any kind of critical choice. Scottie though, while touchingly enchanted by his own vision, realized that at some times its exteriorization was purer, or closer to his intentions than at others.

Scottie exhibited, both in sites of his own choosing and in galleries, in several Canadian cities during the Forties. He was included in the National Exhibition at the Toronto Art Galleries as early as 1941 and, sponsored in that city by the persistent Douglas Duncan, at the Picture Loan society in 1943. He also held exhibitions in Montreal and Winnipeg. In Vancouver, he had, as he preferred, avoided a conventional gallery, and promoted his works himself. None of them was offered for sale, but there was a silver collection to pay his costs and buy new material. 'I've always got a kick out of seeing people enjoy themselves', he told the by-no-means unsympathetic reporter, 'and if I can offer something beautiful to the world I am happy.'

Scottie returned to Britain at the end of the war, probably early in 1945. While he is recrossing the Atlantic for the fourth and final time, I shall take the opportunity to consider the pictures he is bringing with him. 'My work', he was fond of saying, and with every justification, 'is a life's dream.'

3

'A Chinaman does them for me'

Scottie's imagery was in the main limited to comparatively few elements: the sun, plump houses and cities, ponds with swans or ducks on the surface and fish below, trees with birds, imaginary flowers, and two kinds of personages, clowns (himself usually full-face) and the 'Evils' and the 'Greedies' (symbolic and threatening monsters coinciding with moments of tension). Nevertheless, with the aid of these few props, he was able to create a diverse and resonant world covering every emotion from total peace and joy to disquieting anxiety.

In his early work Scottie allowed, or to be more precise was unable to prevent, his personae and objects from milling around at random. From the middle Thirties on, however, they became mostly contained and placed within framed shapes locked within the rectangle of the board or paper on which he materialized them. These shapes took many forms: circular, vase-like, organic or reminiscent of fountains and totem-poles.

There is frequently a degree of metamorphosis. In the magnificent *Self Portrait* of 1940 (pl. 18; the date as always is open to question; on this occasion I would guess it to be several years too late), Scottie's 'clown face' with its sad and knowing eyes and huge, drooping 'fish-scaled' nose is surmounted by an elaborate crown or hat containing a cat-like mask (it is the cone-like treatment of the lines within the mask that makes me feel that the date is incorrect). Two fat outstretched arms, one containing a fish, point towards the edges of the picture. In place of hands they have monster faces: that on the right snake-like with a cruel eye and long tongue, that on the left with a pompous and rather sneering profile. The body is more or less oval, empty at the centre but defined and enclosed by characteristic curlicues and humps approximately echoing each other. The feet, pointing outwards and attached only to very thin points at the base of the body, also double as monsters but slightly more amiable ones. The impact is hypnotic, formally convincing, hovering between comedy and tragedy.

As in much of Scottie's best work (almost all of that executed between the early 'doodling' period and the essentially decorative pictures of the Fifties and Sixties), this fine example gives, at first glance, a sense of two identical halves, like a Rorschach ink-blot test, but on closer examination this proves to be an illusion. Perhaps the intention of creating exact symmetry was sometimes there, but in the event, as in nature where no two sides of a face, no two flowers even of the same species, are exactly the same, so it is instinctively in the work of Scottie Wilson. There is always an organic impulse behind the network of lines, a feeling of growth. For me this is only missing, or at any rate less in evidence, in a series of those completely abstract compositions he executed from time to time. These eliminated all natural phenomena and were built up entirely from elements resembling those discarded pieces of plywood from which an elaborate pipe-rack has been fret-sawed out. He frequently made use of these shapes in his more rewarding work (using them to enclose the empty stomach in the *Self Portrait* for example), but on their own, for me at any rate, they are rather mechanical and arid. Significantly too, they tend to be closest to identically balanced on each side.

Critics have been understandably obsessed with the source of Scottie's imagery. Much emphasis has been given to the Glaswegian fountain (see above, p. 17), justifiably enough in that Scottie himself constantly gave it credence. The other principal element which is inevitably raised is the influence of the Red Indian totem-pole, and here too Scottie was prepared to go along with the suggestion. Indeed, although with more caution than some, I believe that there is something in it. During his Canadian years, Scottie certainly saw totem-poles erected in the public parks and there are strong parallels between their formalized creatures, one perched on top of another, and many of Scottie's pyramid and metamorphic compositions. Eric Lister however pushed it a little far. Having admitted in the opening paragraph of *Portal Painters* that Scottie was 'something of a romancer', he then reports that the artist worked 'as a lumberjack in remote areas', already an unconfirmed supposition. He adds 'here he became familiar with the North American Indians who interested him greatly. He befriended them and learned something of their language, customs and folk-lore.' All of this I very much doubt, although Scottie must have fed it to Lister, either mischievously, or even while temporarily believing it to be true. Much more convincing in my view was what he told Mervyn Levy in relation to the totems' influence on his work: 'Yes, that's true, but the totem poles are my totem poles.'

Other attempts by critics to identify external objects in his work seem to be less viable. His extraordinary imaginary flowers for instance have been equated with those he may have seen in South Africa, his buildings compared with the architecture of India where he served during his early army years. Even Victor Musgrave, in general his most empathetic interpreter, suggests that 'indoors (in Glasgow) he absorbed, with a child's intensity, the patterns of the doilies, the Victorian tablecloths, the lace curtains'. Given the alleged poverty of the Freeman family, I very much doubt that doilies, tablecloths and lace curtains were much in evidence.

Yet it was Musgrave who put into perspective the unconscious transformation of observed reality in Scottie's best work. The sources 'became a part of him, buried somewhere inside him, waiting, maturing, working there until they were needed, when, transformed and transmuted by his poetic vision, they crept fully formed from the tip of his pen'. This appears to me an admirable description of the use to which an automatist like Scottie puts observed reality: a process more or less parallel to the way we dream. The artist himself seemed to be aware of it. 'I go into a trance,' he told Victor, 'and when I wake up they're all waiting for me.' He then winked and made a joke, 'A Chinaman does them for me.' He knew very well how to defend himself.

'... and very rich and distinguished in colour' wrote Mesens and, throughout Scottie's finest period, from the mid-Thirties to the beginning of the Fifties, this was entirely the case. The remarkable thing about this 'richness' was the simplicity of the means with which it was achieved – childrens' crayons which he used with extraordinary subtlety, sometimes under the linked lines, sometimes over them. There is a unique tenderness in the play of Scottie's pinks, blues, yellows and violets as they weave their way through the phantasmagoria of his dreams and nightmares, and yet there is never a hint of sentimentality or prettiness for its own sake. Black, as a colour, he used only occasionally but to great dramatic effect, blocking in large flat areas to form a background, usually when the subject matter has taken a sinister or anxious turn. His greens and browns tend to be sombre, and against them the paler or stronger colours glow as flowers do in nature. It was remarkable too how he contrived colour schemes which were not only individually beautiful, but so orchestrated as to deepen the mood of an image and intensify its resonance. A Scottie Wilson reproduced in black and white loses an integral part of its magic.

On the other hand the given titles of the pictures are not often happily chosen. In Scottie's first major London exhibition, in 1948, E.L.T. Mesens added a severe footnote to the catalogue: 'These works have never been given titles by the artist. Some of his friends have applied titles to a number of the present exhibits but they are either frivolous or pompous

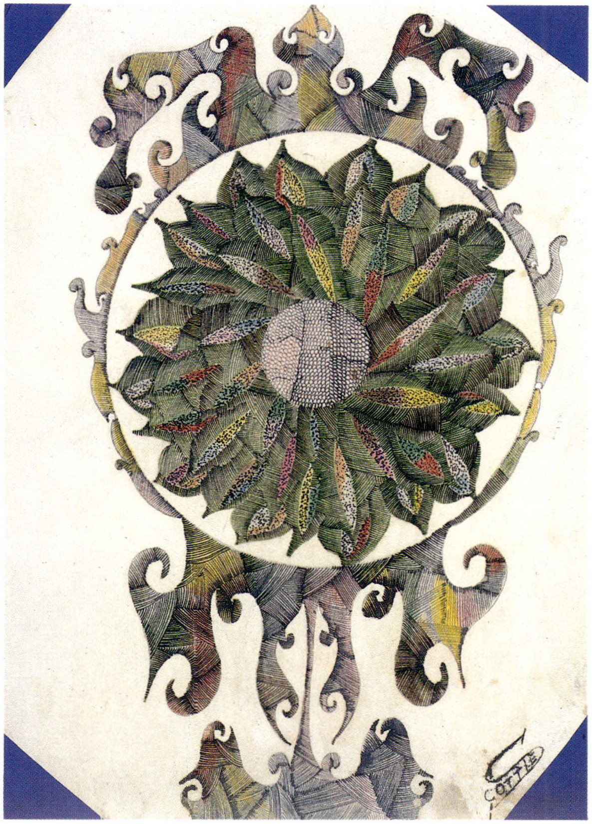

12 Untitled, *c.* 1945. 37.5×28.0.
Gimpel Fils Gallery, London

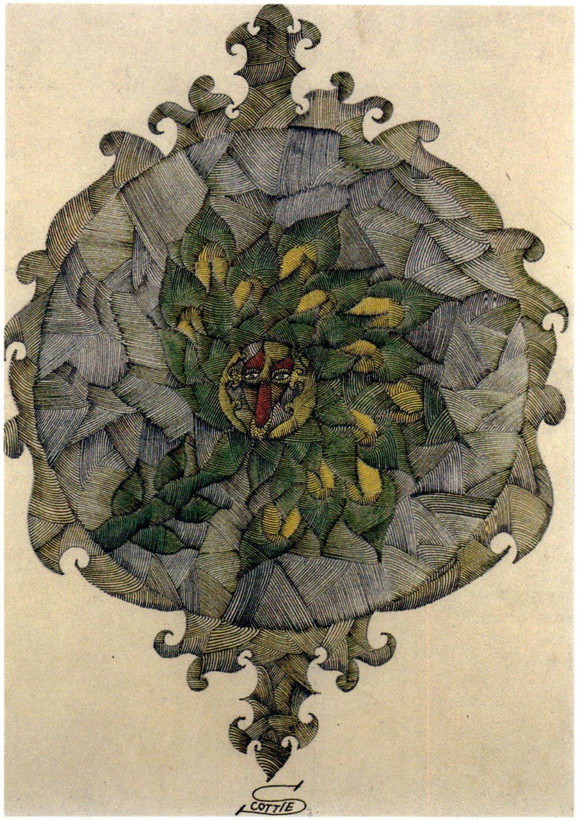

13 *Fantastic Composition*, *c.* 1945. 38.0×28.0.
Gimpel Fils Gallery, London

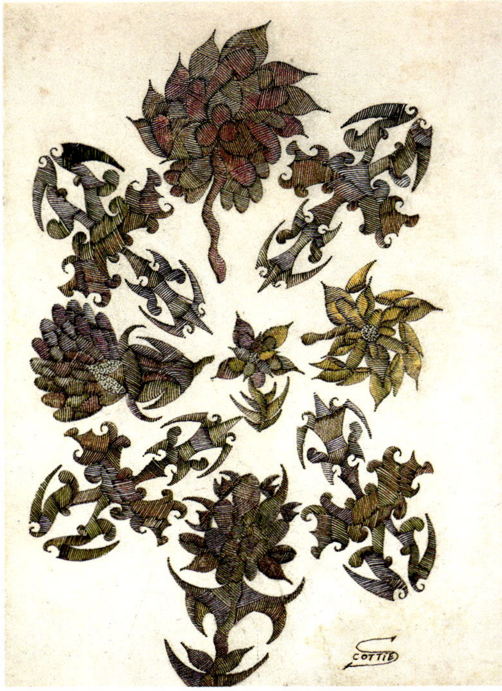

14,15,16 *Top left*: Untitled, *c.* 1945. 38.0×28.0. Gimpel Fils Gallery, London. *Bottom left*: Untitled, *c.* 1945. 38.0×28.0. Gimpel Fils Gallery, London. *Below*: Untitled, *c.* 1945. 37.5×27.0. Gimpel Fils Gallery, London

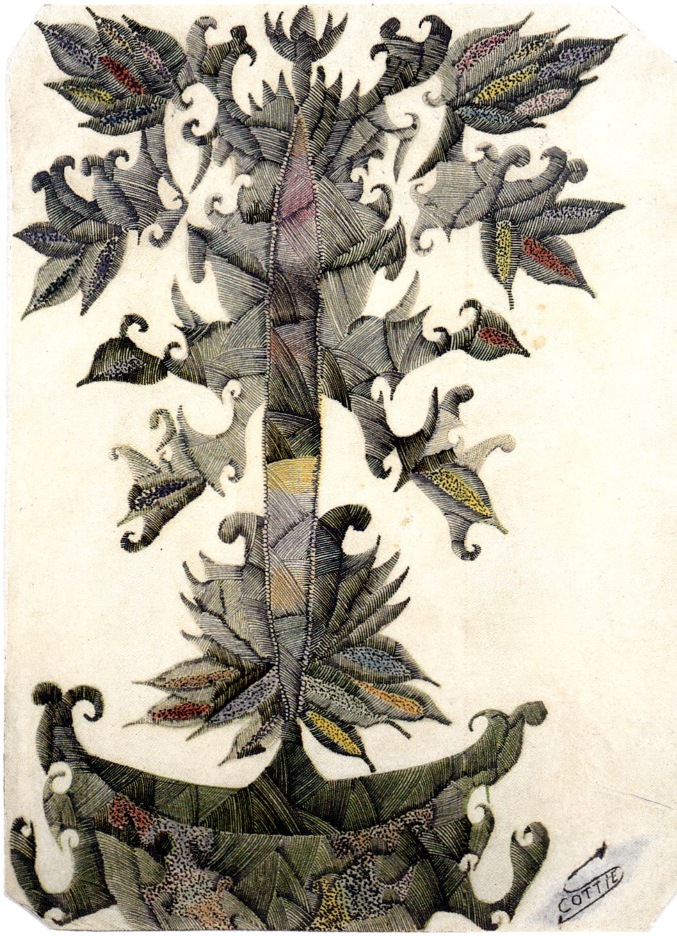

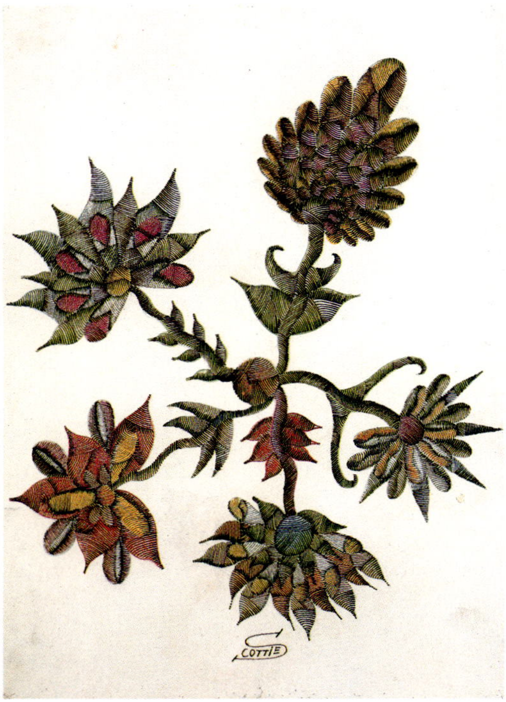

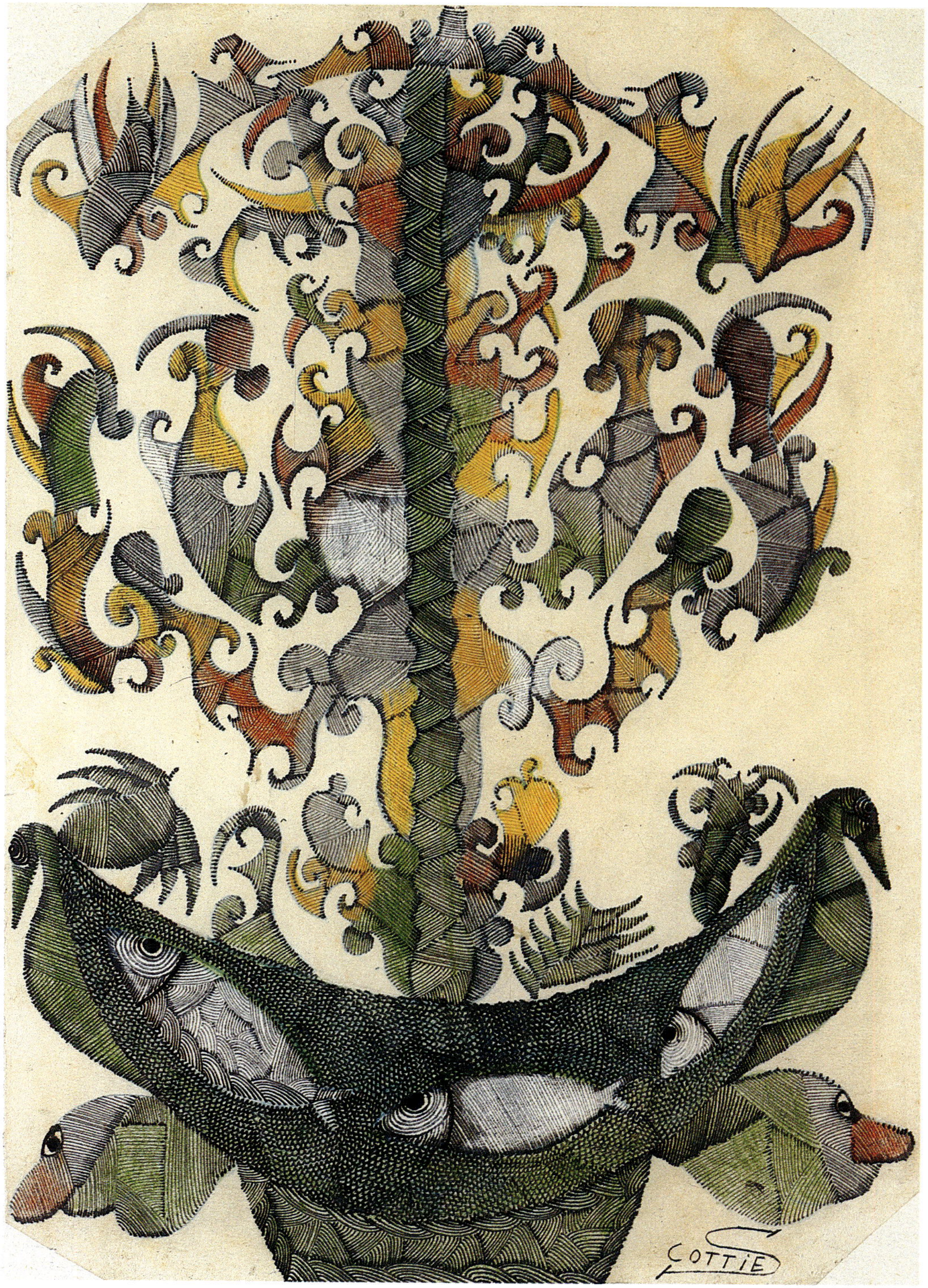

17 *Greedies and Fish Tree*, *c.* 1945. 38.0×28.0. Mercury Gallery, London

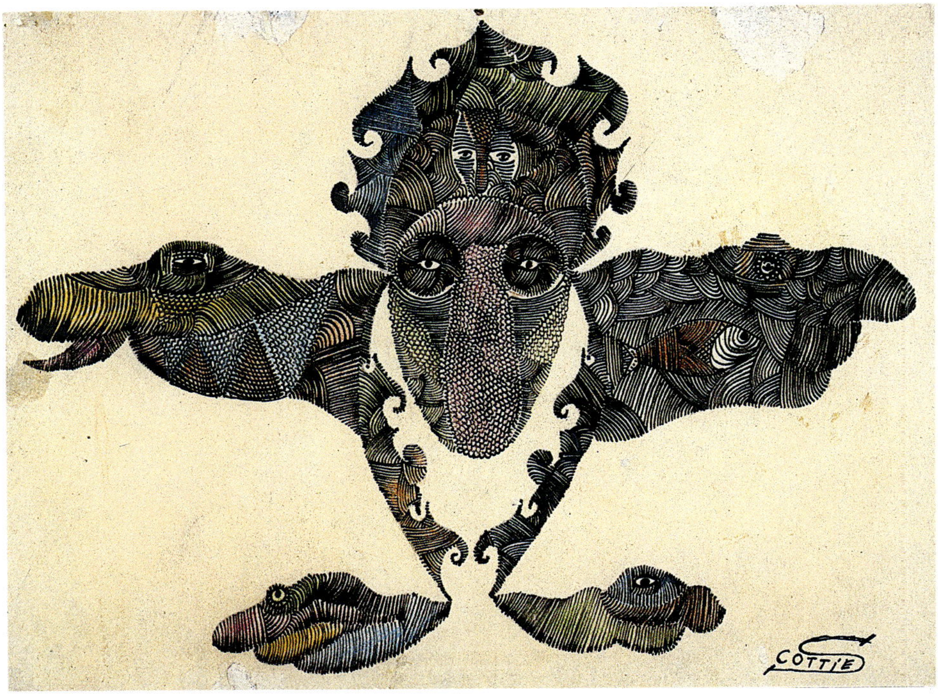

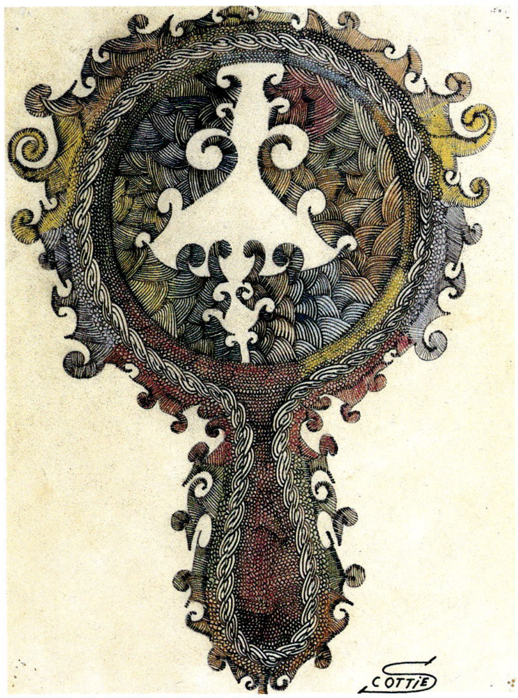

18,19 *Top*: *Self Portrait*, *c.* 1940. 20.3×28.6. Robert Lewin. *Above*: Untitled, *c.* 1945. 26.7×21.0. Mayor Gallery, London, ex Roland Penrose collection

and have not been retained.' This comment itself seems to me a little pompous, but the problem of Scottie's 'titles' is a real one. *Moonlight Mansion, Within Serpents, Sky Totem* and so on I find over-'poetic', on the twee side. The description 'Mind picture' which has been applied to quite a large number of drawings is redundantly obvious. Scottie, unable to read or write, or at any rate not until late in life, certainly would never have submitted titles in advance, although, if *in situ* during the planning of an exhibition, I dare say he may have offered suggestions himself or agreed to those proposed by others. On the whole though it is less distracting when the titles are purely descriptive – *Three Flowers and Two Eyes, Greedies Over a Peaceful Village.* It struck me as quite amusing, considering his stern rejection of titles in the catalogue, that when Mesens published an image of Scottie's as a postcard he chose to call it *Very Tender Tree.* In fairness though, Scottie used the word 'tender' quite often in describing elements in his work, so this may well have been his own contribution.

4

'The moves you make'

The approximate time of Scottie's arrival in Britain is established in the letter which his nephew Alan Freeman wrote to Victor Musgrave in 1984 (quoted above, p. 18). 'Well in 1945 when I returned to England after the war he (Scottie) had just arrived from Canada and was staying with my father (Philip). He asked me to lend him £300 which he would return when his money came through. That was the last I saw of him or my money . . .' Although Victor Musgrave found otherwise, Scottie was not altogether scrupulous about money, but it was usually small sums that he 'borrowed'. Considering the comparatively large amount involved here, the tone of Alan Freeman's letter is remarkably magnanimous. E.L.T. Mesens told another story of Scottie and money, an incident so odd that, far from annoying him, it appealed to his dadaist sense of humour. Scottie asked to borrow a fiver. Mesens, who was beginning to promote Scottie as an artist, naturally obliged. Scottie thanked him, and pulling a large wad of notes out of his pocket, removed the elastic band by which it was secured and carefully added the fiver to it.

We know when Scottie arrived in England, but the true mystery is how, and indeed almost immediately, he established contact with Mesens. E.L.T. is long dead and left no record of their meeting. Sir Roland Penrose died much more recently, just before I had begun to research this book. More tantalizingly, only a month or two earlier, he had recalled an incident which just might have cleared up the question if only I had pursued it at the time. On a trip to Scarborough, he told me, he had visited one of Scottie's self-promoted exhibitions in a deserted wallpaper shop on the front and bought up the entire show. (It would seem that Scottie's resistance to selling his work crumbled when somebody persuasively offered to buy in toto. In Canada, as we already know, Douglas Duncan had acquired twenty-five pictures at one fell swoop.) What is so exasperating is that there is now no way of establishing when Sir Roland bought this collection. If it had been in 1945, it would explain not only how Penrose discovered Scottie but, in that he was a director of the still hibernating London Gallery, how Mesens, its future managing director, would have come to see them, and to meet the artist.

On visual evidence however, I don't think this can have been the case. The Mayor Gallery acquired from Sir Roland towards the end of his life the bulk of this mass purchase and, while several of the pictures are certainly from the Canadian period, others are clearly from the late Forties or even the early Fifties. What Mr Mayor believes is that, with the closing of the London Gallery in 1951, and with no other dealer prepared at that time to take Scottie on, he was very much on his uppers and appealed to Penrose for help. This was forthcoming and says much for Sir Roland's generosity, but still leaves unanswered the question of how Scottie had discovered Mesens some five years earlier. Certainly Scottie's earliest manifestations in Britain were a continuation of his Canadian travelling shows. It is known that he held them in, among other places, Scarborough, Aberdeen, Cardiff, Devon and Blackpool, not only before his 'discovery' by the art-world but long after his work had entered the Tate, the Museum of Modern Art in New York, and many other public collections. It was the presentation of his work he favoured, much preferring it to a more formal setting.

To attract the public he used a gramophone and a loud-speaker. Nothing was for sale but there was a small admission charge and a silver collection. Victor Musgrave, already aware of Scottie from Mesens' article in *Horizon*, and eager to see his work, stumbled upon such a show in a bombed-out shop in Oxford Street (the shop next door was exhibiting Field Marshal Goering's bullet-proof limousine). Musgrave writes:

> Every inch of the walls were covered by unframed pictures held in place by drawing pins. The effect was overwhelming. None of the works seemed to be for sale but there was a plate on a table appealing for a donation of silver. The show was crowded and Scottie moved among the public talking to them about his pictures and drawing their attention to press cuttings which were on display. Scottie advertised these shows with posters. The effect was something between an Indian bazaar – we should not forget that he had been to India – and an elaborate huckster's display...

We should not forget either that he had been a huckster. There is no poster that I know of for the Oxford Street exhibition, but there is one for a show he held in Aberdeen (*overleaf*). Given Scottie's illiteracy he could hardly have designed it for himself, but he may well have dictated its contents. The style, the variation in print faces, the use of question marks and sudden outbreaks of capital letters are late 19th century in impact, but describing himself as a 'primitive artist' suggests that Scottie was prepared to borrow from the despised 'mouthpieces' (as he always referred to intellectuals) when it suited him. The effect however is charming and so, to judge by eye-witness accounts, were the shows themselves. Nevertheless, those 'serious' art dealers who had taken up Scottie were less seduced. If Victor Musgrave had happened to have walked along Brook Street, only a few hundred yards to the south of Oxford Street, he would have found an exhibition of Scottie Wilson, framed and hung on the white walls of the London Gallery. E.L.T. Mesens, despite his Surrealist bias, was not too happy to discover the artist in competition with himself.

Scottie never framed his own pictures for these shows. He covered them very neatly in rather thick cellophane backed with cardboard. The cellophane was slightly opaque and yellowish. When it was removed for more conventional presentation, the beautiful colours emerged with dazzling effect. Scottie's pictures, up until the end of the Forties, were always signed with a large 'S' with the 'cottie' in front of it, cradled in the lower curve of the capital letter. A very few works however carry a rather more elaborate message. They read 'Original free-hand pen-drawings by Scottie', a sentence he must have learned or asked someone to write. The use of the plural 'drawings' on a single picture suggests to me that they may have been so inscribed with a view to pinning them up at the entrance to his self-promoted shows as a guarantee of the unique and genuine nature of the work within. Alternatively he was sometimes upset when it was suggested that his work was so neat that it must have been produced by mechanical means. It was possibly for this reason that he wished to assure that his pictures were all 'done by hand'.

That he favoured a popularist presentation of his art to the hushed ambience of a gallery was something he never concealed. On the contrary: '. . . too good for them,' he told Mervyn Levy, 'too beautiful for this so-called civilisation; too truthful for those mouthpieces. You can't talk to intellectuals . . . they can only hear themselves blabbing a lot of stupid muck. A lot of blah blah. They get paid for it too!' Roger Cardinal confirms Scottie's frequently expressed belief in the superiority of the working class. Of the audience he attracted in Blackpool he remarked appreciatively, 'They're the intellect you know.'

By whatever means he encountered Scottie's work, by October 1945 Mesens had begun to move on his behalf. The London Gallery, which before the war had waved aloft the Surrealist banner in Cork Street in the wake of the great exhibition of 1936, was due to reopen in new premises in Brook Street, but building permits and materials were hard to come by

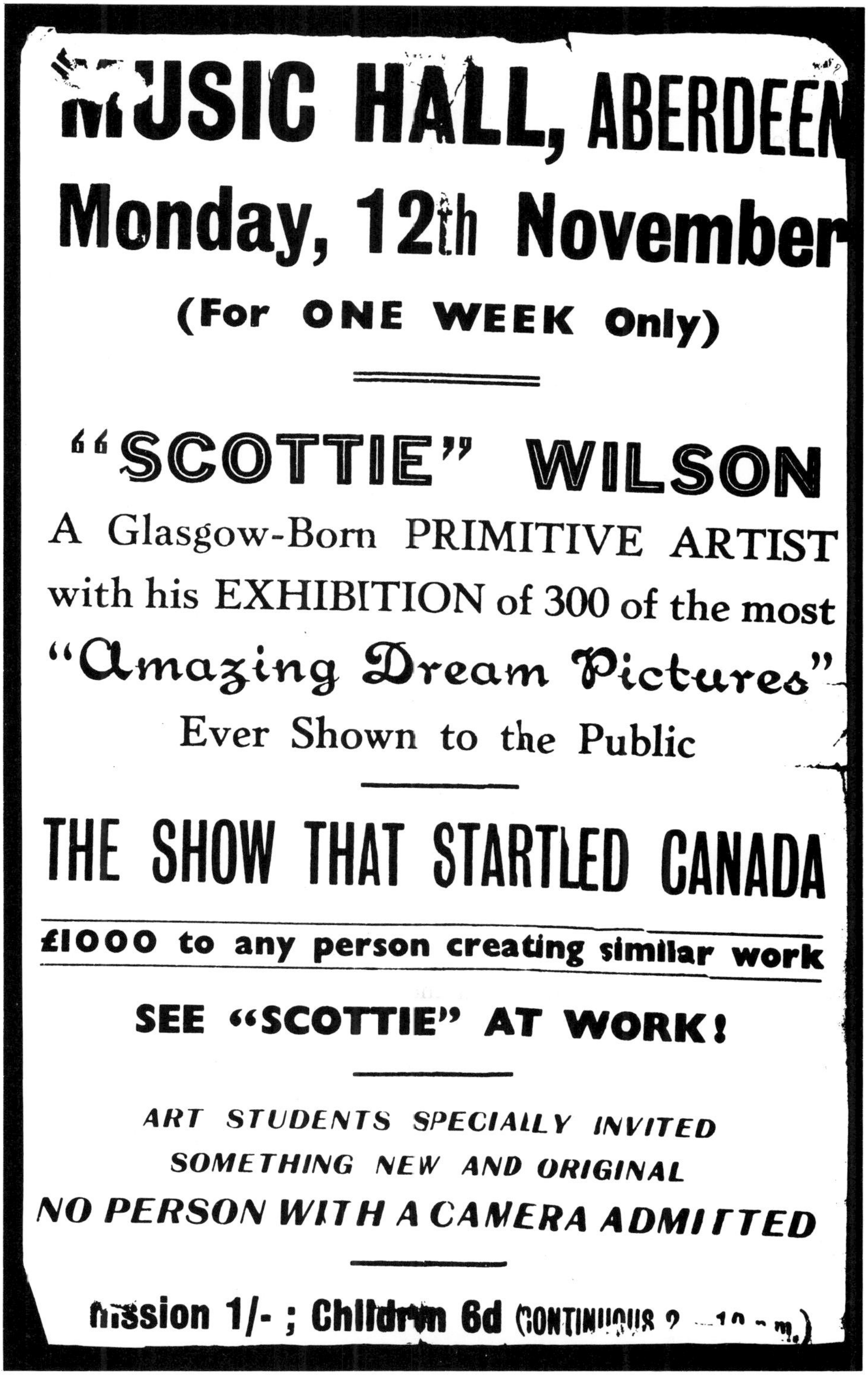

Poster for one of Scottie's own exhibitions, late 1940s

in those austere years and, in the interim, Mesens organized a small but brilliant show called 'Surrealist Diversity' in the Arcade Gallery off Dover Street (18 October–3 November 1945). I was stationed at Chatham in the Navy at the time and paid several visits, very excited to examine original work by De Chirico, Ernst, Picasso, Klee, Miró, etc., artists who, up until then, I knew largely from reproduction. Scottie was also represented but, hypnotized by the 'great names' of the movement and its associates, I cannot pretend to recall his work.

In 1946–7 (December–January), E.L.T. exhibited Scottie's work at the Barcelona in Beak Street, a restaurant which during and immediately after the war served as a meeting place for the Surrealist Group in England. He also took examples of Scottie's work to Paris where the movement, following the return of Breton from the United States, was beginning to re-animate its activities. Breton was immediately convinced by what he saw and included Scottie in the seventh 'Exposition Internationale du Surréalisme' at the Galerie Maeght (1947). Dubuffet, promoter of 'L'Art Brut', was another French convert.

Nor did E.L.T. confine himself to getting the work hung. In the June 1946 issue of Cyril Connolly's *Horizon*, the magazine which above all had kept some form of international culture alive in those dark years, he published his short but admirable article on Scottie Wilson with four illustrations. As a result, by the time Mesens hung forty-six works by Scottie in a show called '3 Types of Automatism' at the London Gallery in February 1948 (it had finally opened its doors in December 1946 with a mixed show including four Wilsons), Scottie was known to the small circle who were interested in the Surrealist ambience which E.L.T. and his gallery were hoping to promote in the unsympathetic climate of post-war Britain.

In the chapter devoted to Scottie Wilson in my book on British naives, *A Tribe of One*, I explained how in late 1947 when, demobbed from the Navy, I was working as an assistant at the London Gallery, Scottie came in to show his pictures and Mesens immediately offered him a show. In that E.L.T. had been exhibiting him since 1945 and had already published his article in 1946, this was clearly a false memory, but I do recall him arriving there with pictures, perhaps for Mesens to make a selection for '3 Types of Automatism' or, more likely, to choose some additional and more recent pictures to add to those he had already acquired (I recall a bundle of 'Scotties' still in their cellophane wrapping which Mesens kept in a trunk).

At all events I was fascinated by the diminutive Scotsman, not only by the stylized appearance, but equally by his gnomic sayings embedded in a stream of consciousness filtered through an almost impenetrable Glaswegian brogue. By this time I not only knew his work, but had acquired two examples of it. I regarded him in consequence with some awe. After a while he and E.L.T. left the Gallery at Scottie's suggestion to go out for a 'wee drink', an activity neither of them was averse to. 'It had taken me', wrote E.L.T. in *Horizon*, 'the greatest patience (and a fair number of pints of bitter) to collect a few facts about himself.'

Scottie was in fact at that time a committed boozer. I remember him at a party given to celebrate *Horizon*'s move to new offices and where presumably he had been invited on the strength of E.L.T.'s article. He seemed an unlikely figure as he stood, becapped and increasingly unsteady, surrounded by the intelligentsia of the period ('Blah! Blah!'). Constantly replenishing his glass with the whisky on offer he finally collapsed. He was helped to his feet by the young Lucian Freud. 'God bless you', said Scottie to his benefactor, 'and God bless your mother!' 'Strangely enough', said Freud when I reminded him of this, 'he did used to visit my mother from time to time, and for the same reason he would visit me, and many other people – to borrow small sums.'

Over the years I was to bump into him at many private views where drink was available and usually by the end of the evening he was obviously the worse for wear. Roger Cardinal wrote that 'he always knew that his attendance at cocktail parties in the galleries was by way of decoration', and so he did, but he knew how to exploit the fact too. It is my belief that Scottie was wily enough as a 'character' (rather than as an artist) to have, as they say now, 'got his act together'. Outside that series of cramped little rooms in Kilburn where he worked with such admirable concentration, he mixed a surprising amount with those 'mouthpieces' he affected to despise, recognizing and very likely playing on that streak of masochism which permeates British cultural life. Alternatively those he frequented – Mesens, Musgrave, Levy, etc. – all of them undoubtedly 'mouthpieces', may have felt that by conferring his friendship, Scottie had excluded them from his general censure. That friendship was not always an unmixed blessing. Taken in large doses Scottie could become repetitive, especially in his cups, but he had an unmistakable gift for phrasing and timing, the equal of those Scottish music-hall comics he, perhaps unconsciously, resembled. There was also the fascination of how, out of that comparatively imprisoned mind, that possibly calculated eccentricity, there could have welled the stream of amazing images described in such a unique, eloquent and totally convincing visual language.

Victor Musgrave gives a description of Scottie's verbal style which, while favourable, indicates its longueurs as well as its points of fascination:

> In conversation he was secretive and evasive, volubly so, about a great many matters, particularly emotions, although he was warm and friendly. He had strong convictions and he held them passionately. He would seldom answer a question with a direct answer, launching into an elliptical monologue which might cover many subjects irrelevant to the question, though it would be in his own mind, and he was working in his own way to answer it. His comments on politicians, experts and bureaucrats was 'Blah, blah, blah', and he was apt to interrupt his main discourse with jokes and muttered asides ('who d'ye think you're speaking to' repeated softly several times, with a sly look, and then he would be off again). The rich Scots accent generated its own warmth. He had a poor memory for names, especially famous ones – although it was quite deliberate that he never got Picasso's right – and little interest in facts and statistics.
>
> His monologues were a kind of instant poetry, studded with reminiscences, jokes, aphorisms on the state of the world, with some of the combined qualities of Will Fyffe, Fernandel and an unsophisticated Mort Sahl. Once started he could go on for hours . . .

This is a loyal and favourable account of Scottie in conversation, but there is none the less a discreetly suppressed hint of occasional ennui in the last sentence.

Musgrave records elsewhere the characteristic entry of Scottie Wilson, almost a materialization one might say – 'I recall the times he has crossed my threshold, diffidently, secretively, unheralded, How often I have looked up to see him in the office doorway, his eyes half moons of impish delight at the encounter. In repose his knobby face seems tired; his smile reveals the undisguised beatitudes of youth. His greeting is typical: "They're trying to get to Mars" he says. "I was there before them!"' There were variants on this theme. After the first moon landing he also reacted by claiming that 'I've been there before them!' In both cases he may of course have been speaking purely metaphorically, but among Victor Musgrave's notes I came across a pencilled query on a small single sheet of paper. 'Was Scottie a schizophrenic?' The answer would seem to be no, but is it possible that he was kept sane through his exteriorization of those very fantasies which might have overwhelmed his sanity?

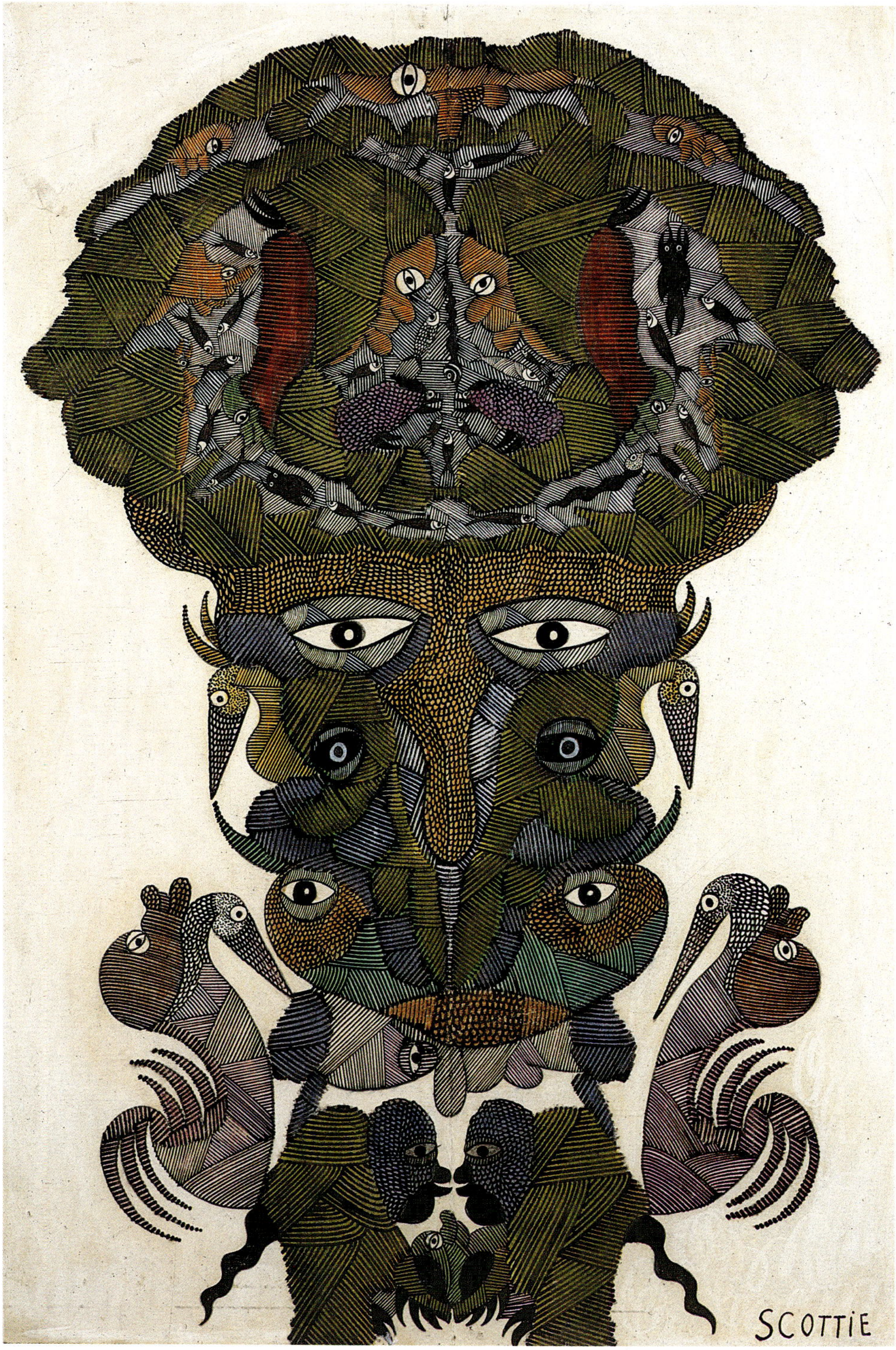

20 *Greedies II*, 1950s. 45.5×32.0. Gimpel Fils Gallery, London

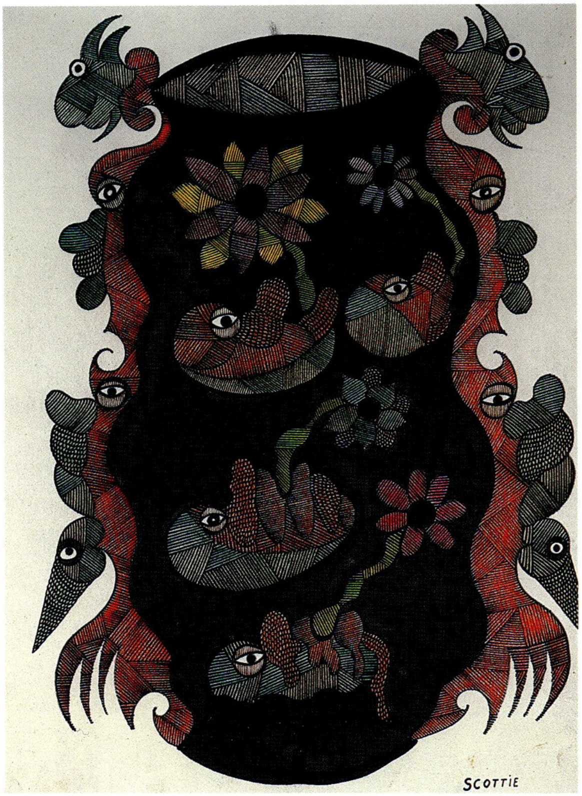

21 Untitled, late 1940s. 36.8×27.3.
Robert Lewin

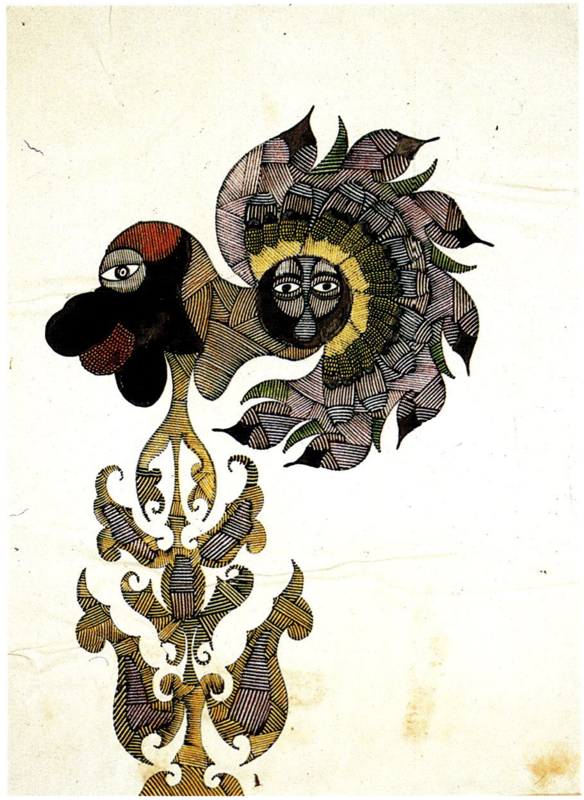

22 Untitled, late 1940s. 37.0×28.0.
Lee Miller Archives

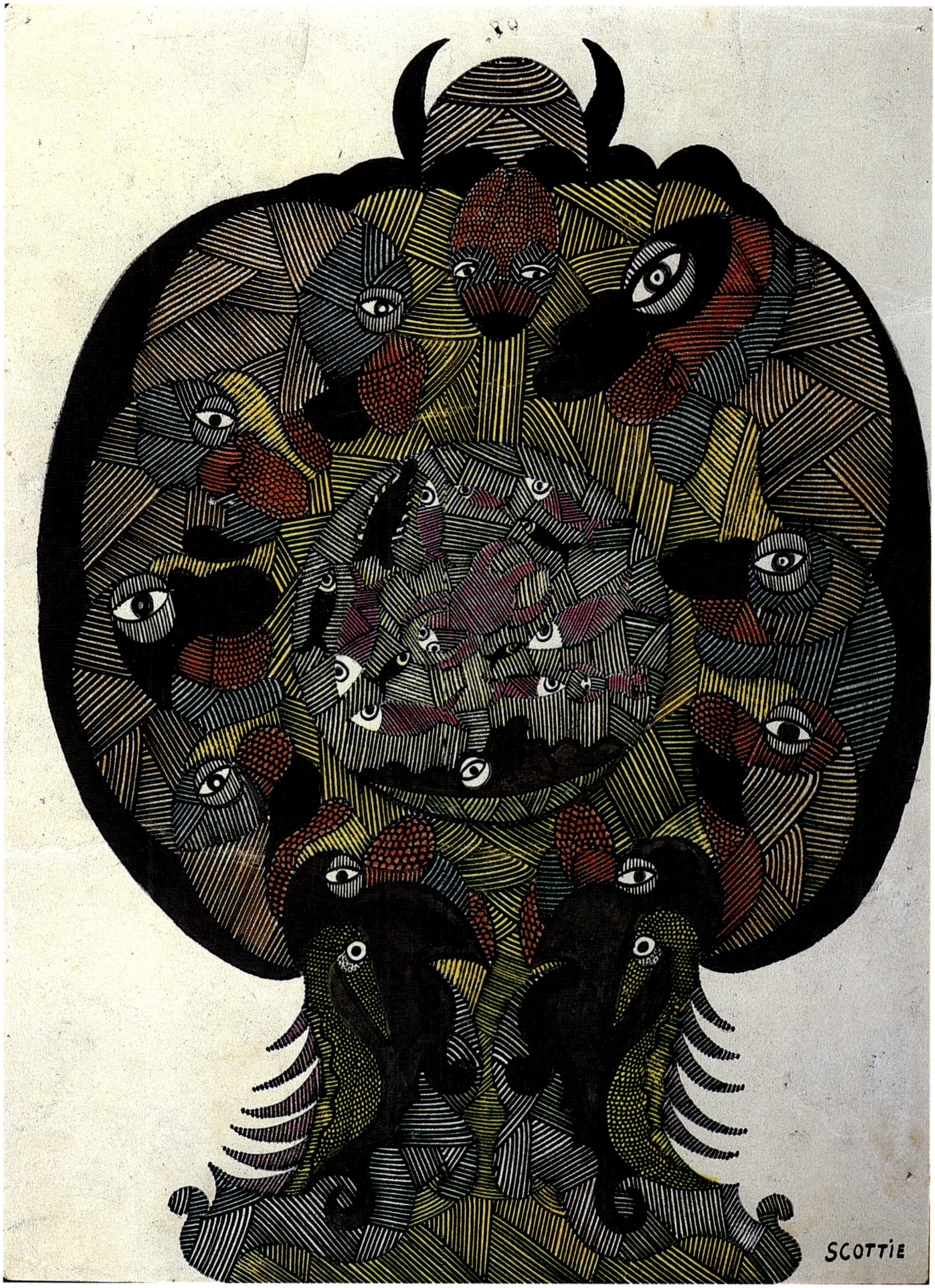

23 Untitled, late 194cs. 38.0×28.0. Robert Lewin

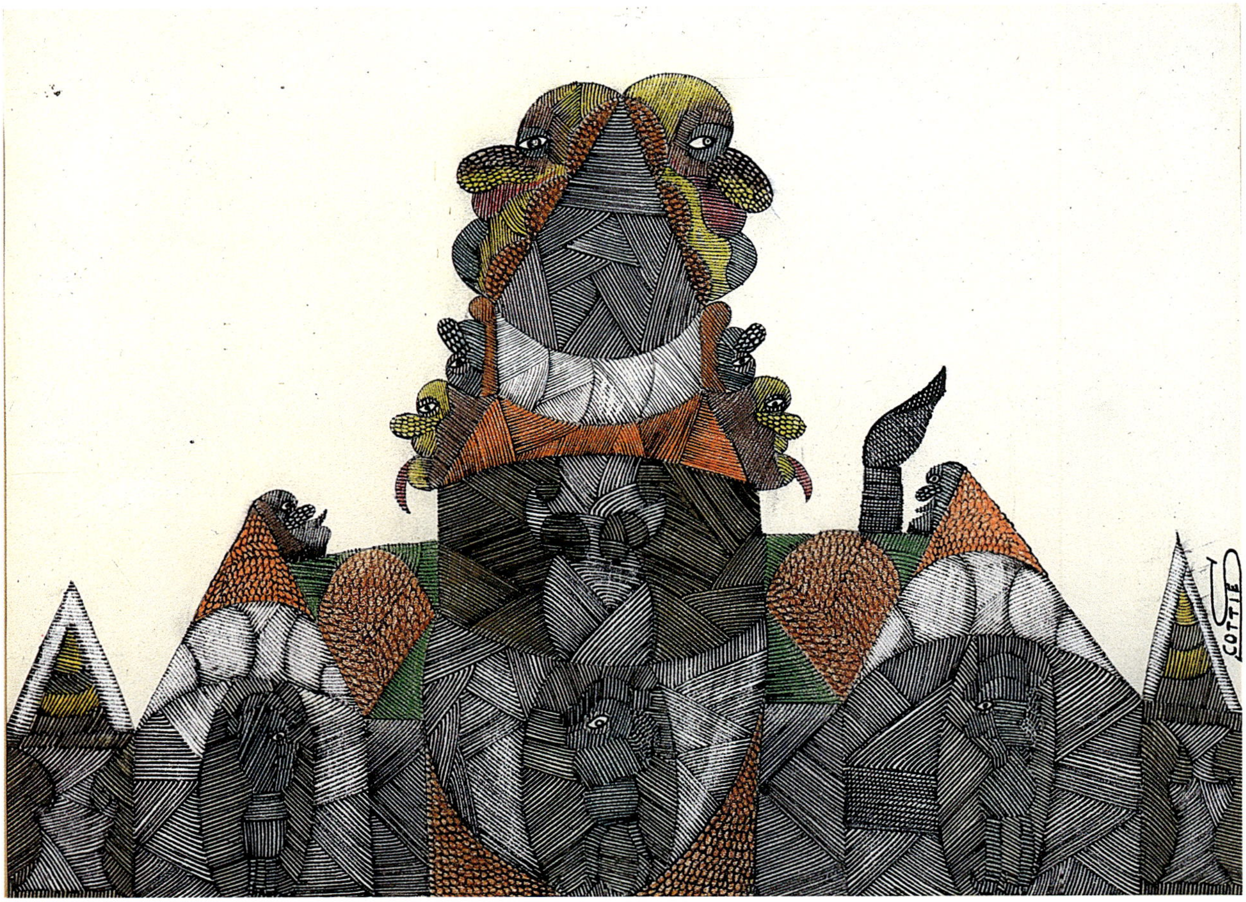

24 *Greedies Threatening a Peaceful Village*, *c.* 1950. 38.0×27.3. Robert Lewin

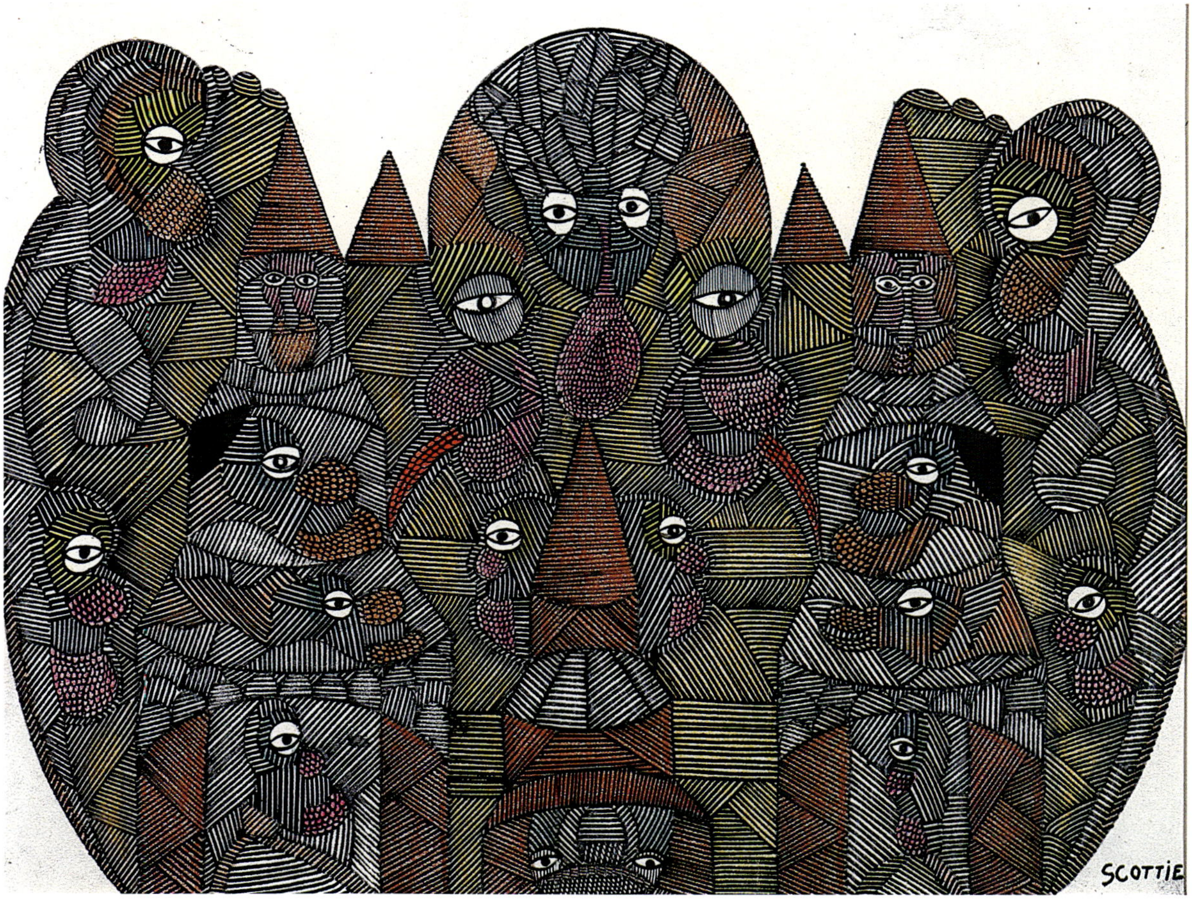

25 Untitled, *c.* 1950. 27.3×36.8. Robert Lewin

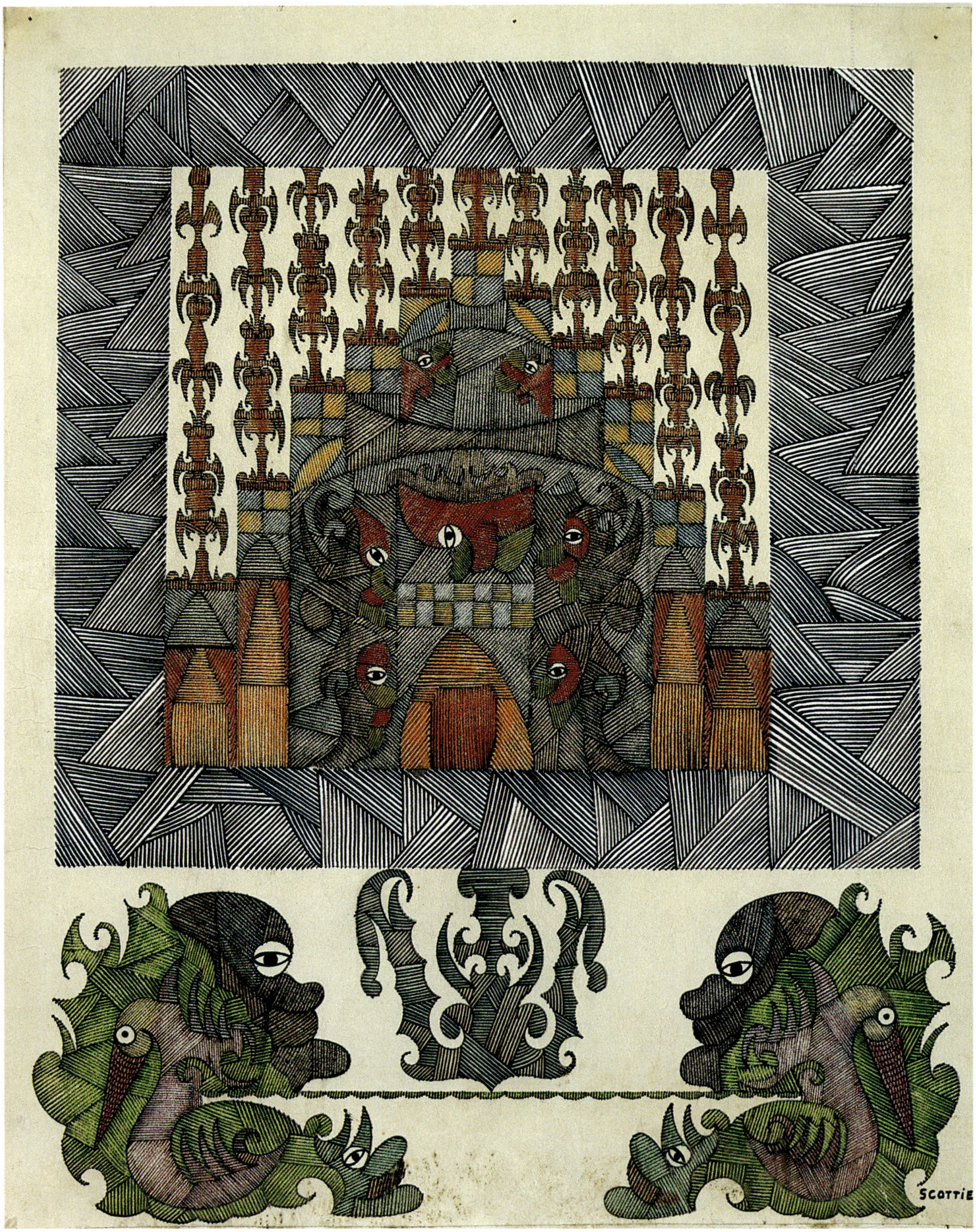

26 Untitled, *c.* 1950. 65.0×49.0. Lee Miller Archives

Of the value and beauty of his work he had no doubts. 'D'ye think the angels don't know my work? They love it, and when my time comes I'm ready for a good talk with them. I'm looking forward to meeting Willie Blake too.' Blake he quite frequently mentioned, usually in the same breath as 'Rabbie Burns'. The latter is quite predictable. Is there a Scotsman whether by birth or, as in Wilson's case, by adoption who doesn't pay at any rate lip-service to the national poet? 'Willie Blake' though is more problematic. Scottie, besides being illiterate, told Mesens that he had never met an artist until he began to draw and became recognized. The only vaguely 'artistic' moment he could recall was the result of his meeting in Toronto a man he called 'The Professor'. 'This man', Mesens reports, 'was dirty and badly groomed, and very unhappy with his "missus". When the "Professor" started to play his fiddle the wife shouted and locked him in the cellar. And there the violinist could apparently only obtain from his instrument the most horrible catcalls – except when "Scottie" accepted to go into the cellar with him and conduct (!) his playing. Then, apparently, they had great moments of "artistic exultation".'

So where did 'Willie Blake' come from? I suspect from an admirer or sequence of admirers of Scottie's vision who either compared him to Blake, or insisted on showing him examples of Blake's work. The lovers of primitive painting tend to be unable to resist this kind of thing. It's a dangerous activity, threatening exactly the self-taught spontaneity which is presumably what they treasure in the first place. Even Mesens was guilty of it. 'I have put him in front of paintings by artists as diverse as Miró, Picasso, Chirico – even purposely in front of two beautiful Paul Klees – and his answer was a polite "very nice".' It's as well for us it was. It would have been a tragedy if Scottie had become no more than an imitator of Klee. Scottie, although uneducated, was no fool. Blake's 'otherness', his visionary dottiness and private mythology offered Scottie a way to 'explain' what he was up to, to shut questioners up. Musgrave says Scottie was aware of other artists and spoke admiringly of Turner, but he never enthused over a contemporary, with the exception, according to Mesens, of Magritte. Besides Burns and Blake, the only other members of Scottie's pantheon were Moses, Einstein and Charlie Chaplin. 'Believe me,' he once told Musgrave, 'the only people who are civilized in this world are you, me and Charlie Chaplin.'

That Scottie, cunningly, should have protected himself and his art by accepting or even promoting a handful of acceptable explanations put to him over the years by helpful 'mouthpieces', is almost certain. In regards to the Indian totem-poles he usually conceded their influence or even promoted the idea, but to Mesens who met him so soon after his return to Britain, it was a different story. 'Strangely enough, when I asked him if he remembered any American Indian art he did not, and found no comment to make on them. Perhaps he had absorbed them with his inner eye.' Perhaps indeed!

5

'This wicked world'

Scottie's defence mechanism also covered his illiteracy, his lack of education. On the one hand he was defiant about it: 'Perhaps I can see as clearly as I do because I ran away from school.' 'Thank God I ran away from school.' 'My mind is reading all the time. I don't need papers or books. My mind is full of books.' On the other hand he could resort to mild deception to conceal his illiteracy. 'In the thirty years I knew him', wrote Victor Musgrave, 'he would sometimes hand over to me a letter or other document, asking me to read it to him "as I've left my spectacles behind".' Musgrave was puzzled that he should have occasionally carried a *Daily Mirror* in his pocket. 'He may have been able to glean something from the headlines and photographs', he concluded.

Schreiner, in his admirably suggestive essay, treats Scottie's illiteracy as a positive advantage:

> Scottie could neither read nor write, which might almost be interpreted as a deliberate stance. One could almost say revolutionary. But let's not go that far. He has placed himself on the periphery and has all the appearance of being wise. To be a wise man in our time no longer consists in accumulating knowledge, but on the contrary freeing oneself from it. Wisdom consists in getting rid of the acquired in order to become free to choose. The times are gone when wisdom was based primarily on the accumulation of knowledge in its broadest sense. Knowledge has deliberately been diverted from its objectives. What we call rational today encompasses but an infinitesimal part of knowledge. The biggest part, what we readily call irrational, because it is disquieting, is only the mirror of our ignorance. It is infinite.

Although frequently and eloquently dismissive of intellectuals in general and art critics in particular, Scottie was less specific about other objects of scorn. He did however hold all politicians in fine anarchic contempt: 'Politicians! My God! They should have my beautiful truthful pictures all over that House of Commons, then they could talk about civilization!' Indeed 'civilization' was a constant source of rage and despair for Scottie: 'This so-called civilization!' 'This cock-eyed civilization!' 'This wicked world.' He did believe however that somehow, sometime, things might improve, that the Garden of Eden, purged at last of the 'Greedies' and the 'Evils' would be restored to us.

Roger Cardinal reports how Scottie's 'indictment of "this rotten world", "this cock-eyed civilization"' was 'followed by a moving statement of his confidence in the possibility one day – perhaps as much as a hundred and fifty years from now, but certainly sometime – of a regeneration of mankind, an entry into a new order of things in which a wise simplicity will obtain in human relations and a true "civilization" will emerge.' He could joke about the future too. He told Mervyn Levy, who asked him what the world would be like in a couple of hundred years, 'Oh! It will be a wonderful place – for anyone that's got my pictures, that is!' Not that it was a total joke. Scottie believed that his vision, even when it touched on the struggle between light and darkness, between good and evil, was a reflection of an ideal world, possibly a future world. 'When I'm working I can see what's happening, and I can imagine what's going to happen. I can see best when I'm finishing my pictures with a pen. When I'm making strokes; hundreds and thousands of strokes. I can see then very clearly . . .' (in conversation with Levy). One is reminded here of those mantra which mystics use as a way of emptying the mind, of self-hypnosis and, less reverently, of Mesens' masturbation theory.

Scottie's optimism about a new golden age was not always so sanguine. He told one friend, Conrad Wilson, 'I know what's happening and what's likely to happen. I don't want to tell you about it. It might frighten you!' Perhaps that day the 'Greedies' and the 'Evils' were in the ascendancy. Levy asked him once if he believed in God. 'His answer was categorical. "God? – of course I believe in God! – who else should I believe in? Macmillan? Khruschev?" '; a rather tenuous theological argument. It was also one of the few times, to my knowledge, that he mentioned specific contemporary figures. In general his world was peopled only by archetypes; dark forces opposed by redeeming resilient nature. Always excepting of course 'them fellows who would know what I was getting at' – Robert Burns, William Blake, Moses, Einstein and Charlie Chaplin.

6

'The people mostly cannibals'

Immediately after his arrival in London in the mid-Forties, Scottie moved into the first of a series of small rented rooms in Kilburn, a rather seedy itinerant working-class area much favoured by the Irish, and, except when he was away organizing one of his self-promoted exhibitions, it was to remain his base until his death in 1972. Not that he would appear to have had any particular fondness for the district; 'Kilburn is a jungle', he would mutter from time to time, 'and the people are mostly cannibals.'

As he grew older, and began to earn a steady income by the sale of his pictures through the West End galleries, his provincial expeditions became less and less frequent until they petered out altogether. He had taken to showing his pictures in an old bus, but in Cardiff, where he stayed for some time, it was always being moved on by the police, and in Devon, on the very last excursion he made, it broke down irretrievably. From then on, cannibals or no, he stayed put except, rather surprisingly, for several trips to France, where he had become a friend of Dubuffet, and to Switzerland.

His routine was set. Mervyn Levy, who visited him in the early Sixties, described how he rose at any time between four and six a.m., pottered around until the eight o'clock news and then went back to bed for an hour. From nine until twelve-thirty he worked. Then he shopped, prepared and ate his lunch, slept in the afternoon, worked in the evening and went to bed between midnight and one a.m. He would punctuate his day, Levy explained, with coffees at one of Lyon's restaurants in Kilburn High Road, and an endless chain of Woodbines.

His basic diet was eggs, cheese, kippers and chicken. 'You can get a lovely piece of chicken for two shillings', he told Levy. 'First I make chicken soup, after which I've still got the chicken to eat cold.' Kippers he always claimed to be his favourite nourishment, even in the London Gallery days. He mentioned them often, as though they were as much a part of his persona as the cap and muffler, a kind of prop. They've always had a slightly music-hall aura anyway, and I suspect Scottie was aware of this. There was also whisky, at one time in some quantity, but as he grew older he drank less and less. He grew to be more of a recluse also, paying only rare visits to the West End galleries. A lonely existence on the surface, but then Scottie had his work. In his neat bleak room stood a table and seated at it hour after hour he lived his real life.

He exhibited regularly. The London Gallery, its cellar full of Surrealist masterpieces nobody wanted, closed its doors in 1951, but Scottie, after a short if disastrous hiatus, had no difficulty in placing his pictures, especially after they became more accessible and decorative. He showed in London at Musgrave's Gallery One, Gimpel Fils, the Brook Street Gallery, the Arcade Gallery, the Fieldborne Galleries and the Ben Uri Gallery. Posthumously, up until the time of writing, his work has been seen at the Mercury Gallery, the Mayor Gallery, and there was an important retrospective at the Artists' Market in Covent Garden. His work has also been exhibited in Paris, Basel, Zürich, Brussels and New York. He didn't have to go short of kippers in his later years, and could well afford to indulge his sardonic little joke: the purchase of a 'typical' working man's cap, and a muffler and boots from the most expensive shops in Mayfair and St James's.

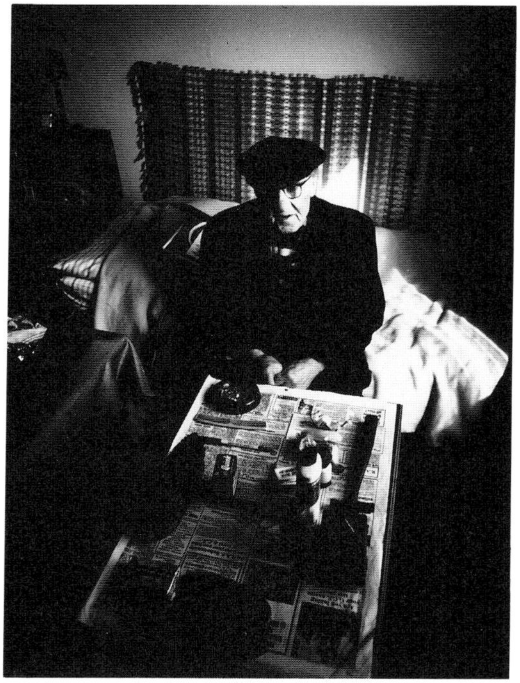

Scottie in his room in Kilburn, April 1966.
Photo: David Hurn/Magnum

Never unsuspicious of exploitation, of having one 'put over him', he became increasingly difficult to deal with as he grew older. Kay Gimpel, wife of the late Charles Gimpel of Gimpel Fils, told me that it was particularly frustrating to try to explain their financial dealings with him because, in concealing his illiteracy and near-innumeracy, he would become more and more agitated, sometimes to the extent of running off into the street, where he would try to sell his pictures to passers-by for nominal amounts. Dr Myerson told me that he was perplexed (or perhaps pretended to be perplexed) as to why this so upset his galleries. 'I don't see why', said Scottie, 'they can't sell my pictures for what they want and I sell them for what I want.'

The owner of the Fieldborne Galleries in St John's Wood gives an example of his behaviour towards the end on his life:

> During his last exhibition, about three months before he died, we decided to have a late opening one evening. He arrived earlier than arranged and had to wait. He upbraided us in his penetrating gravelly voice, but he must have regretted his behaviour because the following day he came with a peace offering of candied fruits for my wife.

It doesn't seem too heinous a lapse to me, but then of course I don't know the manner or matter of the upbraiding.

Certainly as he grew to be old, he became even more of a recluse, obsessively rigid in his self-imposed routine. The minor operation for hernia and prostate was entirely successful, but Scottie was upset by the separation from his environment, by the antiseptic imposition of the alternative discipline of hospital life. It threatened his omnipotence. He became increasingly intransigent and aggressive.

Scottie's life divided almost exactly into two halves. For his first forty years he was exposed to the rough-and-tumble of the world; impoverished childhood, the army, second-hand dealing. During his second forty years he was an artist, a solitary by choice, engaged in revealing over and over again some aspect of his inner world. He hid also behind his stylized 'auld working chap' image and his stock of aphorisms: 'If there's one thing the world loves – it's a bargain and a scapegoat.' On the other hand he was totally indifferent to his reputation, showing no interest in any article written about him, however favourable, nor much pleasure in the fact that more and more people appreciated his work. He took that as his due. Kay Gimpel told me that, if he was in the gallery and she introduced him to someone who had bought one of his pictures, he would forestall any praise or interest with the dour phrase 'Very wise.' Nor did he seem to be aware of any art except his own. 'In the gallery', said Kay Gimpel, 'he never lifted his eyes to the wall.' He appeared unconcerned about his prices. He himself would sell his pictures for very little, especially in bulk. Only during his last few years, according to Victor Musgrave, did he suddenly demand large sums for them. Perhaps he feared a drying-up of that stream of images which had flowed for so long.

Despite his dislike of art critics ('they're just jugglers – dodgers'), Scottie, while sometimes patronized or pigeonholed over-glibly, was not too badly treated by them over the years. There was however the case of Evelyn Waugh, not in itself important in any final analysis of Scottie's worth, but almost inevitably brought up by his defenders, and discussed by them with such inaccuracy and incomprehension that I feel it is worth turning aside for a moment to set the record, as I understand it, straight.

It has, in reality, very little to do with Scottie as such. It is more directly concerned with the love-hate relationship between the great novelist and Cyril Connolly, editor of *Horizon*, and thus publisher of E.L.T. Mesens' article on Scottie Wilson. Waugh was an unrepentant reactionary who included amongst his many other 20th-century bêtes noires, modern art in general and Picasso in particular. He was also a tease. His nickname for Connolly was 'Smarty-boots', and it was that love of teasing him which formed the basis of the Scottie Wilson 'case'.

In the opening chapter of *The Loved One*, an extremely funny and apposite satire on 'the American way of death', the hero, a rather unpleasant English poet, is visiting the Hollywood cricket club, last refuge of the British colony. He has with him a copy of *Horizon*. One of the old crocks, once a fine writer, now a studio hack, examines its contents and the following dialogue takes place:

'Kierkegaard, Kafka, Connolly, Compton-Burnett, Sartre, "Scottie" Wilson. Who are they? What do they want?'
'I've heard of some of them. They were being talked about in London at the time I left.'
'They talked of "Scottie" Wilson?'
'No. I don't think so. Not of him.'
'That's "Scottie" Wilson. Those drawings there. Do they make any sense to you?'
'No.'
'No.'

And that was it. Naturally enough Waugh, whose taste lay in the direction of the Pre-Raphaelites and Victorian narrative painters, would

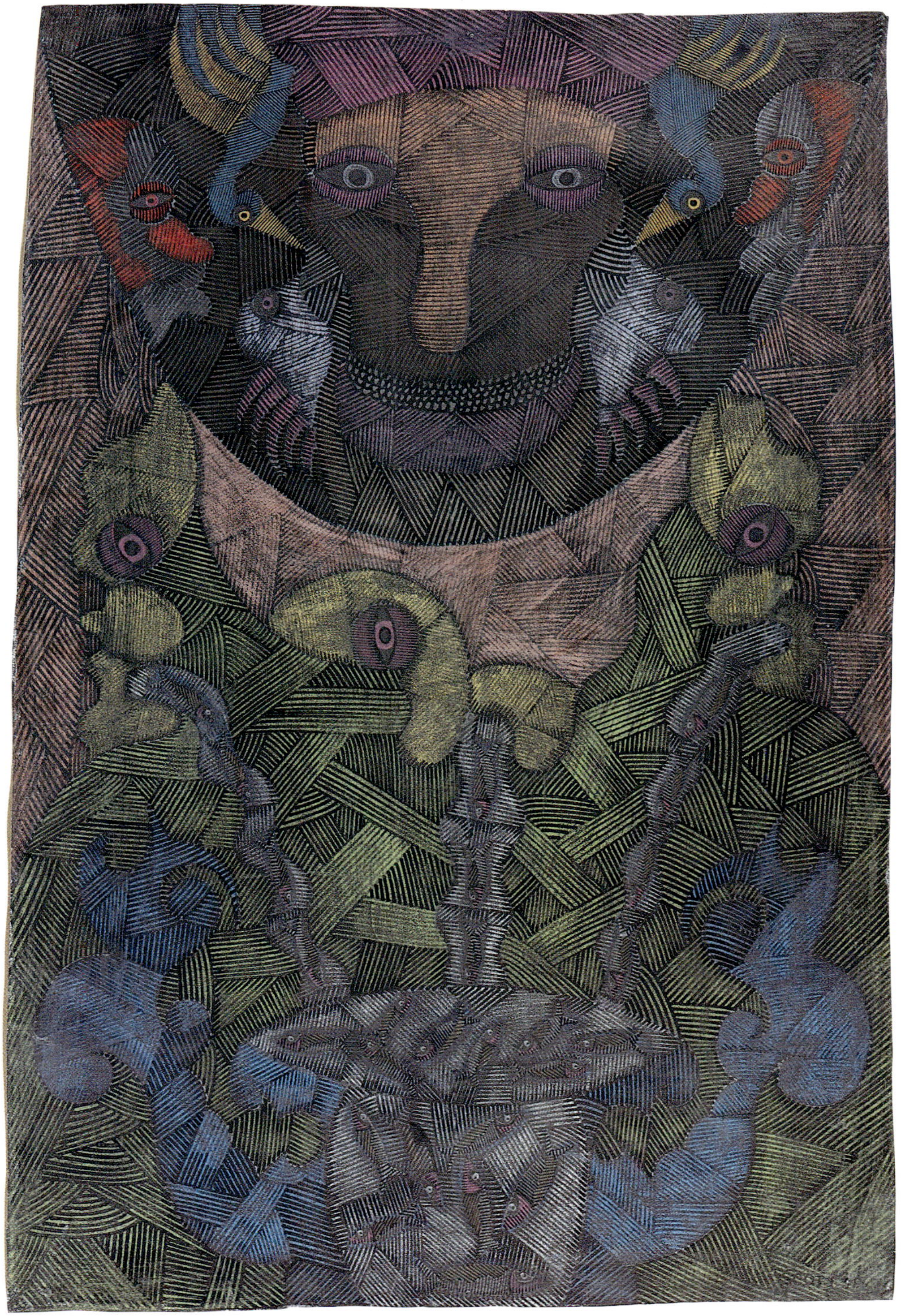

27 Untitled, *c.* 1950. 48.6×33.3.
Mayor Gallery, London, ex Roland Penrose collection

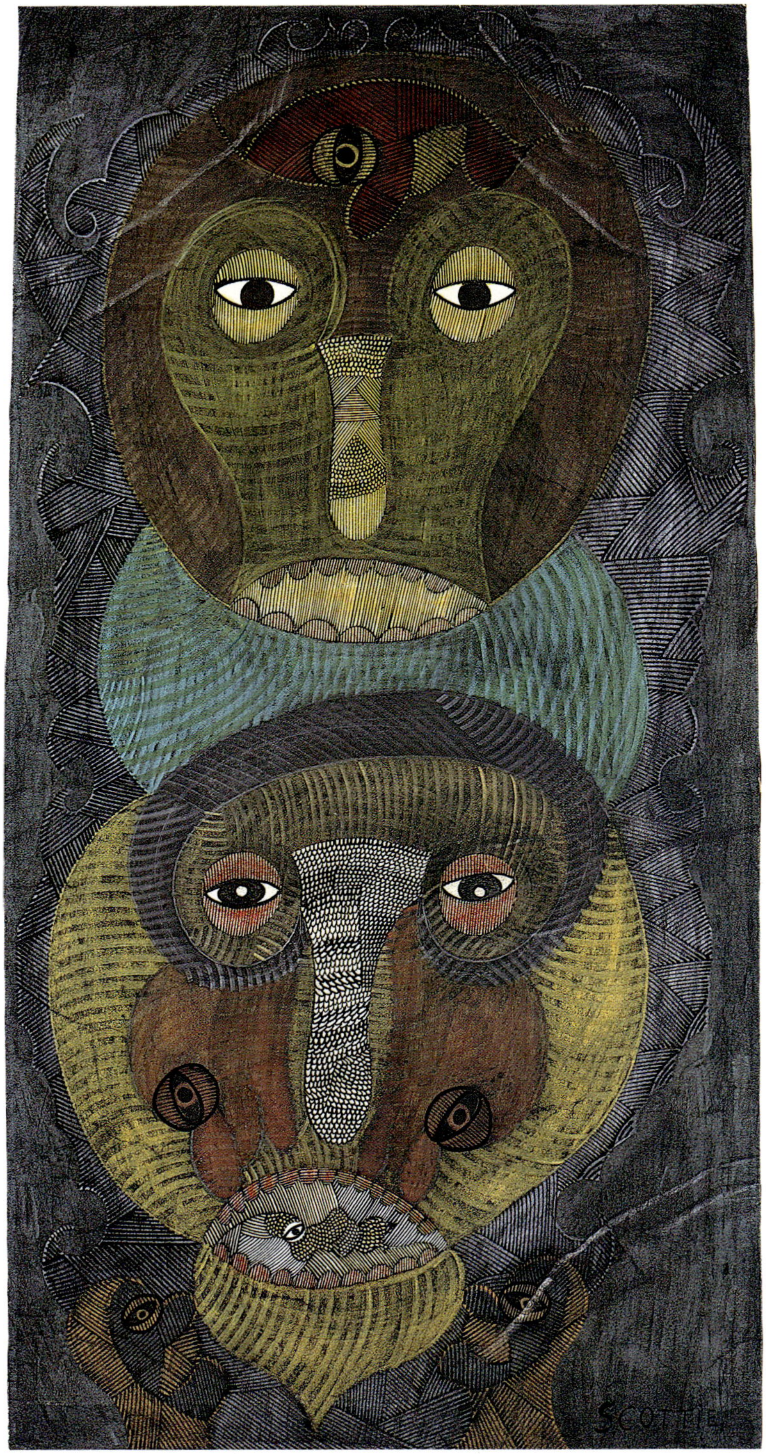

28 *Overlapping Heads*, *c.* 1950. 53.2×28.0.
Collection de L'Art Brut, Lausanne

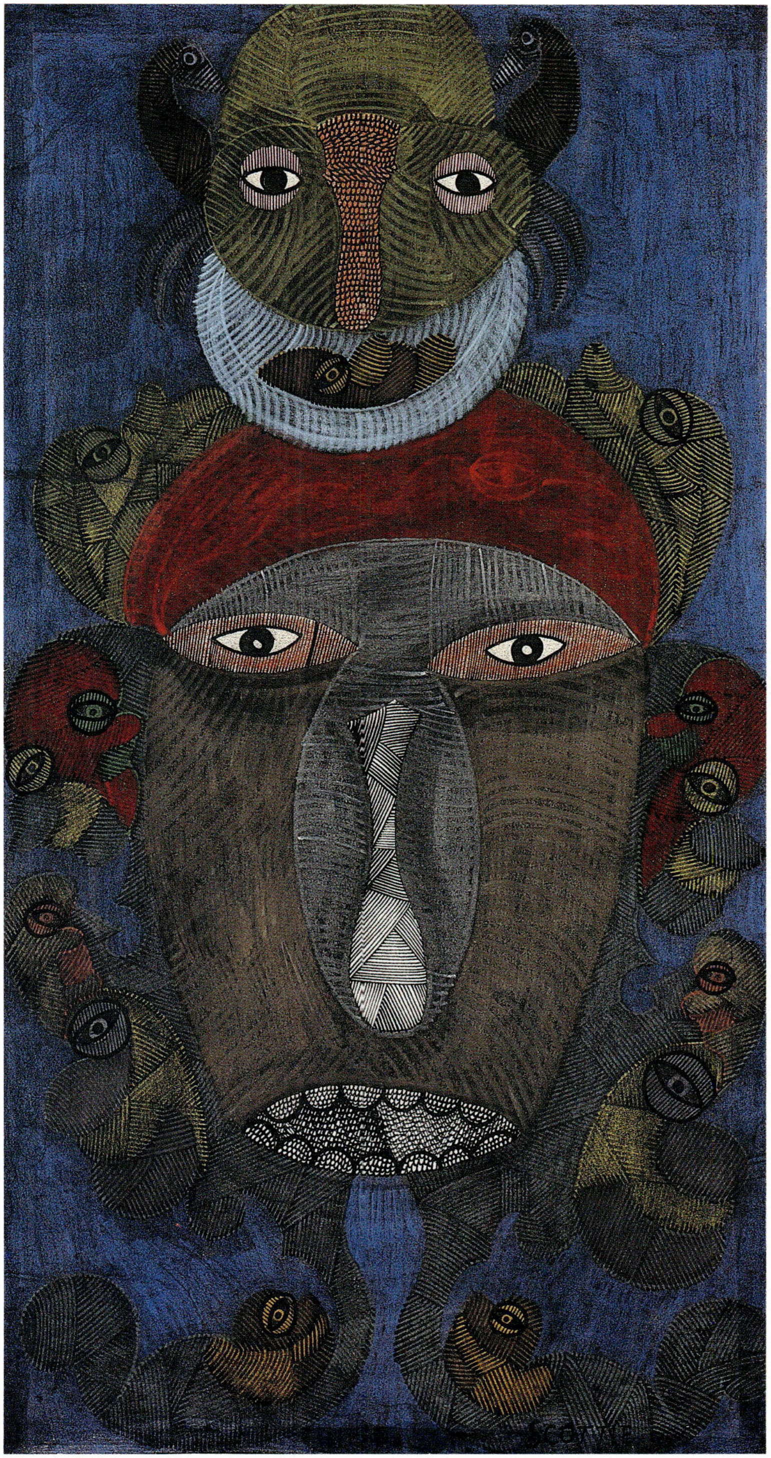

29 *Two Figures with Pink Eyes*, *c.* 1950. 51.0×27.5.
Collection de L'Art Brut, Lausanne

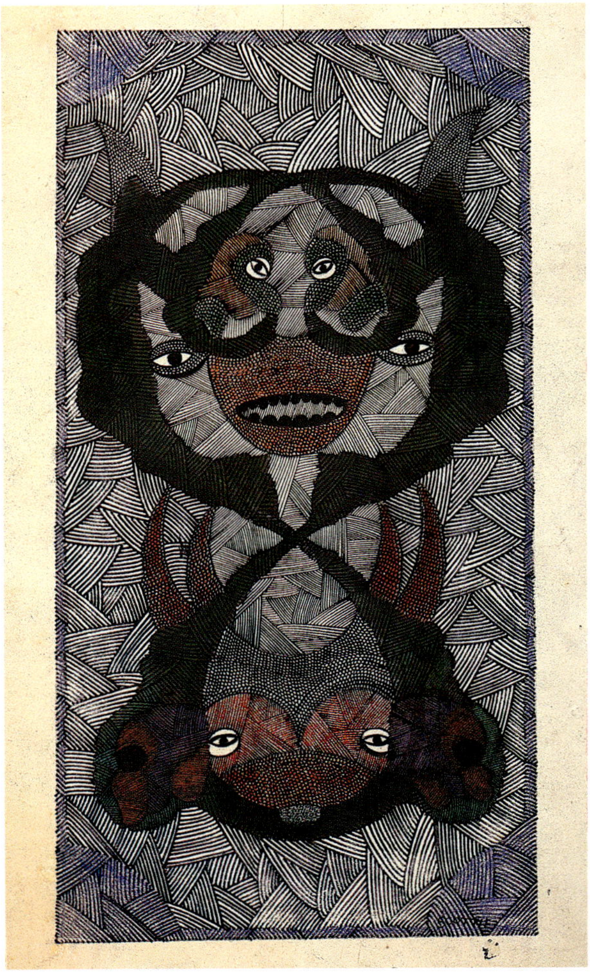

30 Untitled, *c.* 1950. 38.7×20.3. Robert Lewin

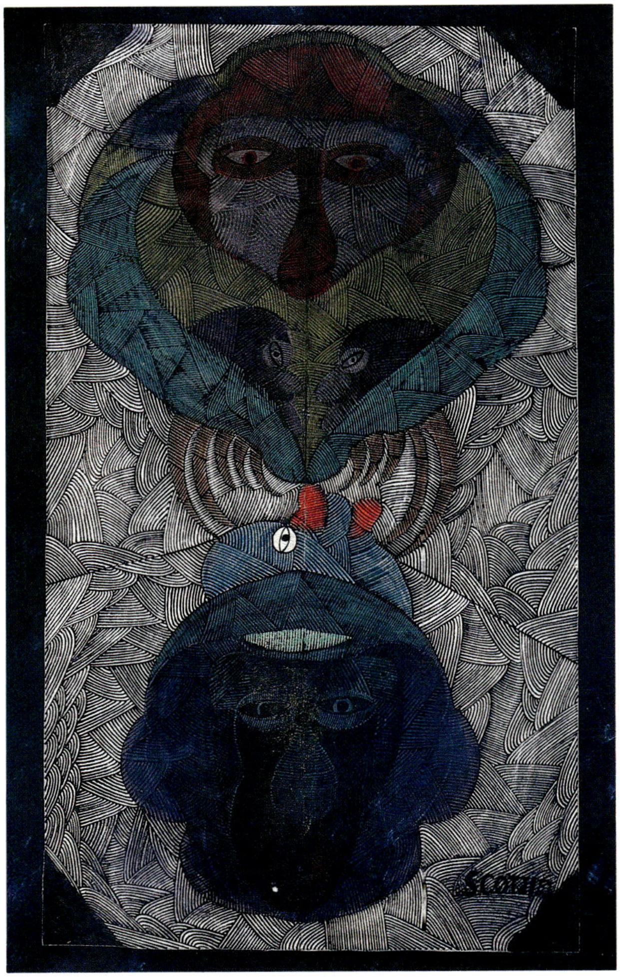

31 Untitled, *c.* 1950. 43.8×26.0. Robert Lewin

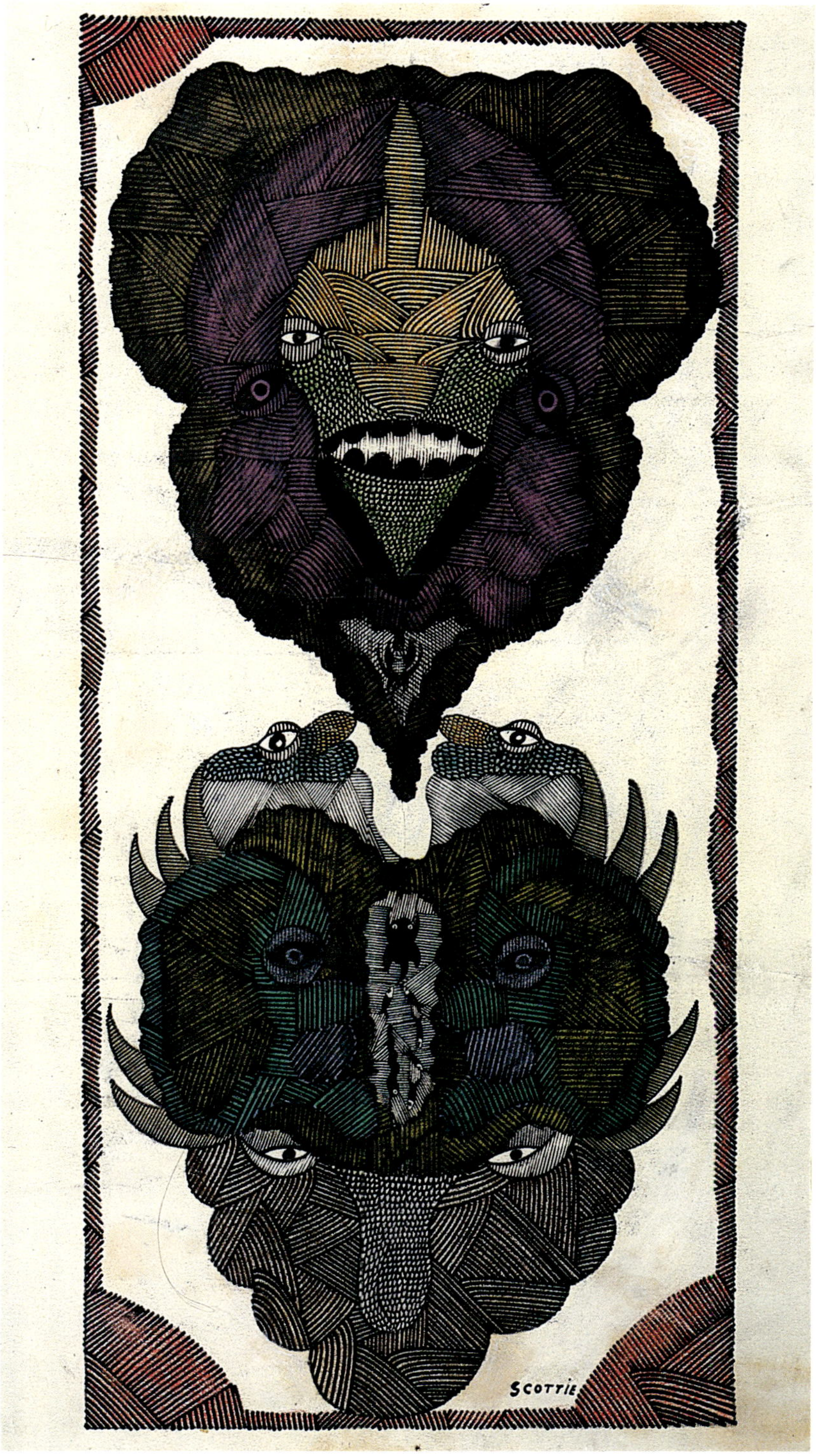

32 Untitled, *c.* 1950. 43.8×20.3. Robert Lewin

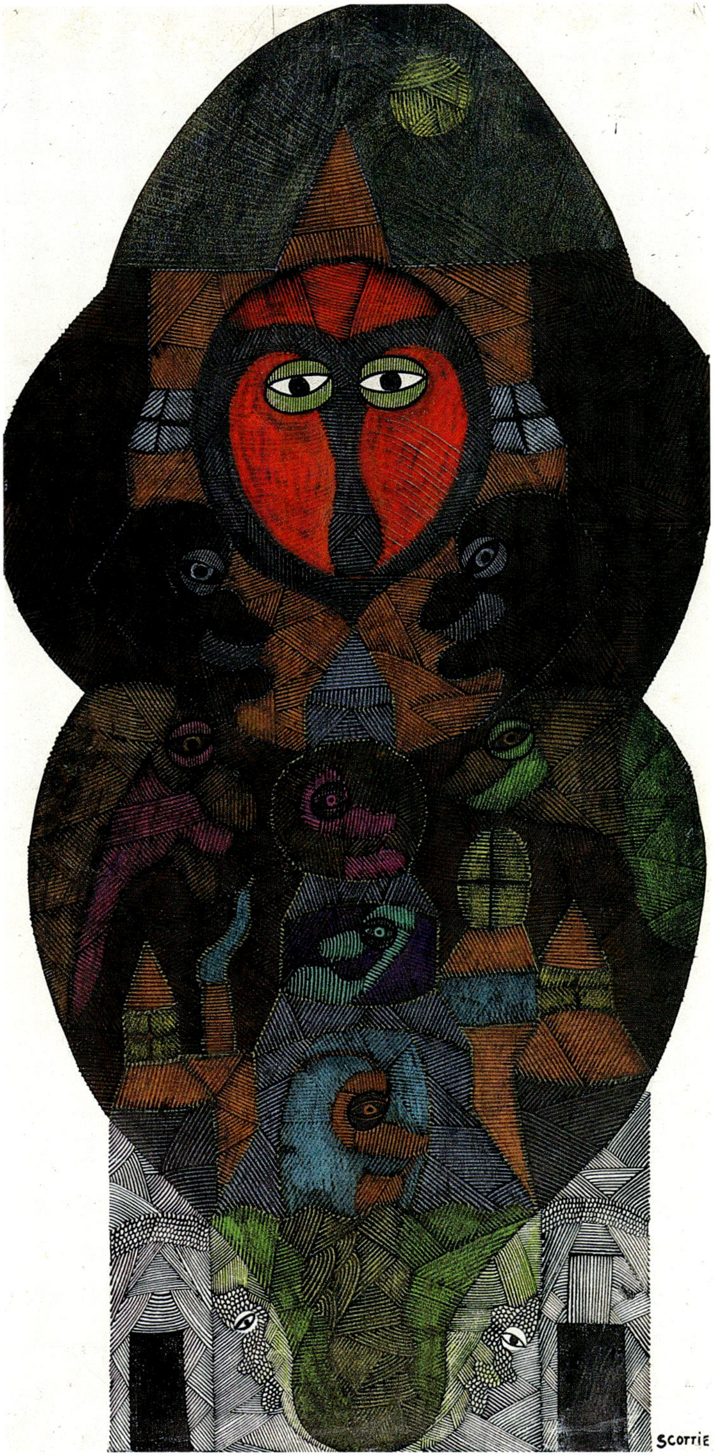

33 Untitled, *c.* 1950. 58.7×29.2.
Mayor Gallery, London, ex Roland Penrose collection

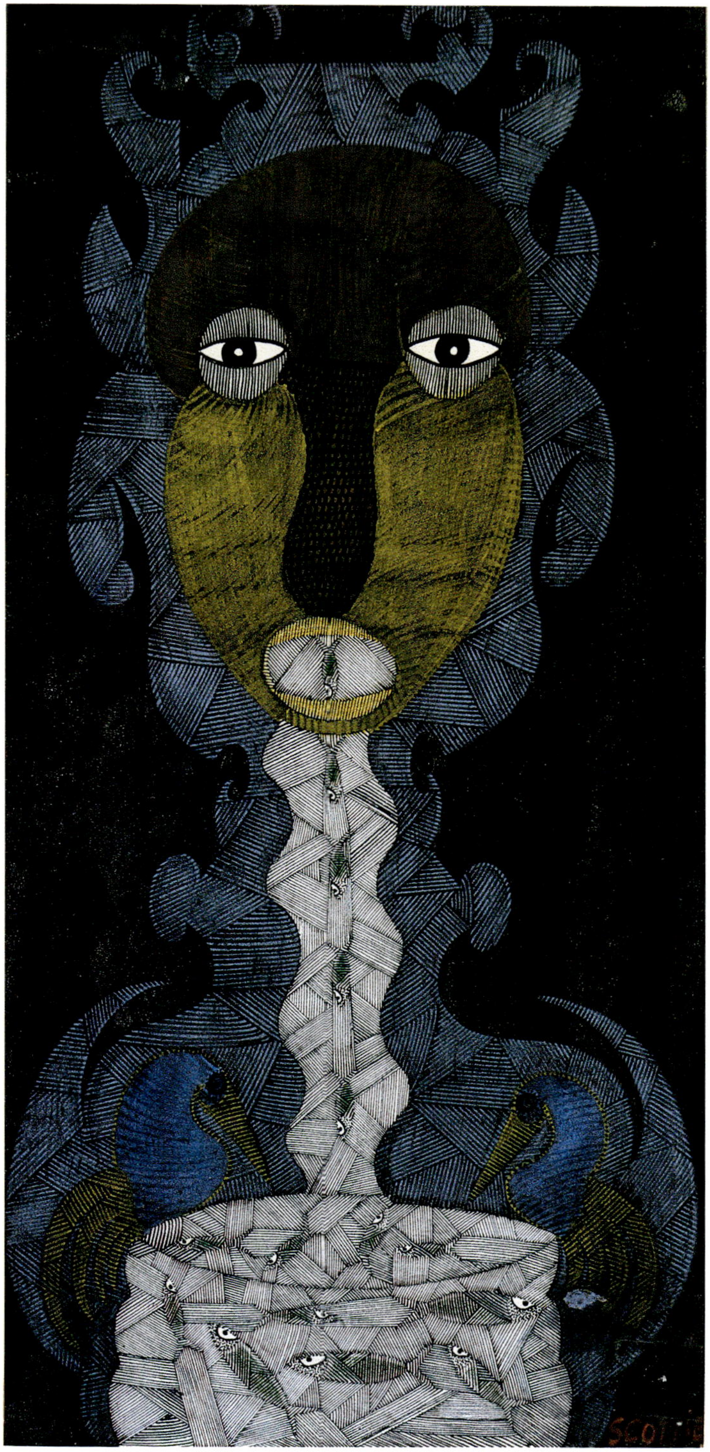

34 *Fish Eater*, 1950. 53.0×27.0. Lee Miller Archives

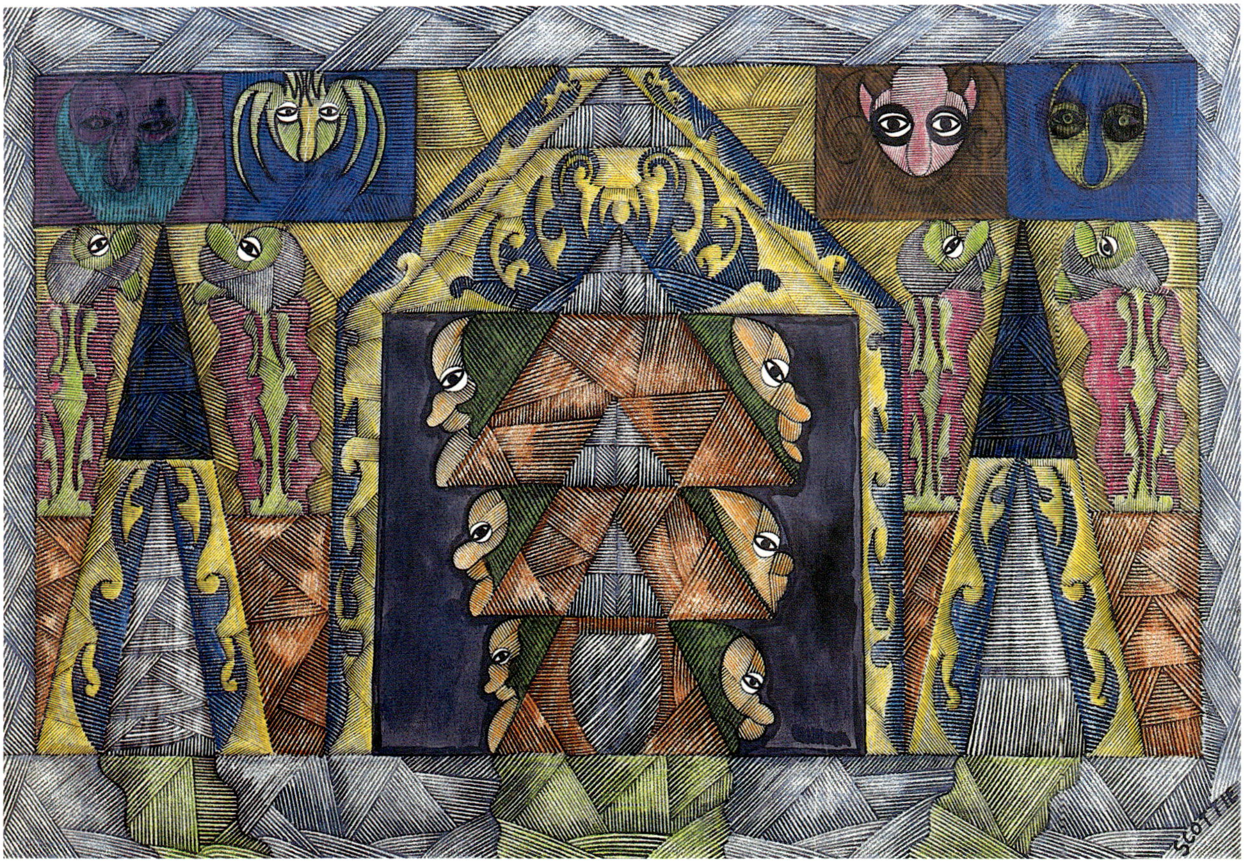

35 Untitled, early 1950s. 36.8×53.3. Mayor Gallery, London, ex Roland Penrose collection

have found Scottie not at all to his taste, but the main target of his satire was the contents as a whole of a typical number of *Horizon* and his intention was to give mild discomfiture to 'Smarty-boots'. To rub it in he offered *The Loved One* to Connolly, who was of course delighted and indeed obliged to devote a whole issue to it. Nor was Waugh, at that time, inaccurate. Not many people in London 'talked of "Scottie" Wilson'. E.L.T. Mesens' article to which Waugh refers was in fact Scottie's first mention in the British press.

Nevertheless this harmless little joke has tended to produce an over-reaction among Scottie's defenders over the years. Victor Musgrave for example wrote: 'A peculiar reference to Scottie's work by Evelyn Waugh in *The Loved One* strikes a jarring note, Waugh makes one of his characters call Scottie "a bright young thing who is all the rage".' Waugh does no such thing, and I'm rather surprised that Victor, who was always meticulous in his research, did not look it up to see what he did write. Compared however with Gérard A. Schreiner, Musgrave is pedantically accurate:

> In a novel "the loved one" [sic], famous in its day [still famous and rightly so, G.M.], Evelyn Waugh put the following words in the mouth of an insipid and disillusioned character who holds in his hand the classic whisky and soda: 'Kierkegaard, Kafka . . . "Scottie" Wilson – who are they? What do they want?'
>
> This literary event took place several years after the war and that brief passage – without any apparent significance – was enough to get Scottie discovered by the professional discoverers. He was an overnight sensation and found himself on the brink of a great career . . . The experience soon led Scottie to call a halt, to the great dismay of the grave-diggers of Culture.

This farrago of nonsense, especially odd in that Schreiner's essay is on the whole so full of insights, has not even a vestige of truth. *The Loved One* was published by *Horizon* in February 1948 (it was to come out in book form later the same year), that is to say in the very month that Scottie exhibited at the London Gallery. There was no 'overnight sensation'; the few pictures he sold were to those already convinced by the Surrealist spirit. The exhibition was hardly noticed by the press. It was to be some years before Scottie achieved even a small reputation, let alone 'a great career', although Waugh continued to tease Connolly about him. Where on earth did Schreiner derive his entirely spurious theory? Anyway the last laugh is on Waugh after all. People do and will continue to 'talk of "Scottie" Wilson'.

Never one to relinquish a running gag, Waugh in a letter to Connolly dated 16 September 1947 suggested that, in exchange for publishing *The Loved One*, Connolly should 'put a guinea or two in "Scottie" Wilson's begging bowl'. In his reply Connolly reported that 'Scottie Wilson has come to London . . . only to experience the ingratitude of the dealers and fickleness of the public. He is now quite destitute and lives on small loans of up to ten shillings a time from Lucian Freud. Shall we really give him some guineas from you?'

Most of this was nonsense. Scottie never left London during this period other than to promote his shows in the provinces for a few months at a time. Freud, as we know, told me that Scottie did indeed occasionally 'borrow' ten shillings and sometimes visited his mother ('God bless your mother!') on a similar errand, but then, as the story of Mesens and the five-pound-note suggests, the artist frequently asked for loans when he had no need of them. The late Forties were in fact a comparatively prosperous time for Scottie. The London Gallery showed him, and Mesens had stimulated an interest in his work both in Paris and elsewhere. It is possible that after the Gallery closed its doors in the early Fifties he may have gone through a bad patch, but even then Penrose's mass purchase would have got him out of trouble, and there was not much of a gap before other dealers took him up. Scottie's material needs were few and, while somewhat paranoid about financial dealings, he was not unastute. What temporary set-backs he experienced were usually the result of his self-prompted provincial ventures.

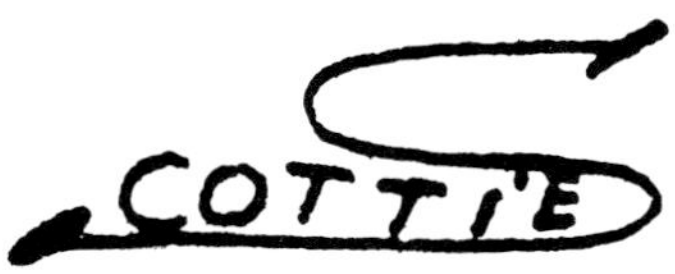

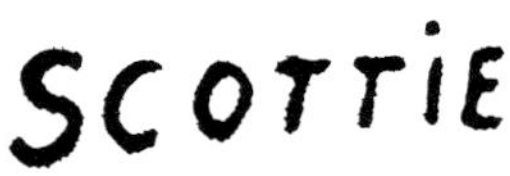

At some point, probably after his return to England, Wilson changed his signature, dropping the large 'S' with 'cottie' in front of it in favour of 'SCOTTIE' in neat and equal letters. At approximately the same time some of his images began to spread outwards towards the edge of the picture space and so to assume the form of a conventional landscape, although for quite a time these alternated with his more customary vase-shapes, ovals and totems.

Towards the end of the Forties there were rapidly increasing signs that Wilson was going through some psychological crisis, that the 'Greedies' and the 'Evils' were winning. In his earlier and largely Canadian work, while menacing enough, they were held in check. Now the defences were crumbling. The means he used were still the same: crayons and black ink, but there was a noticeable coarsening and broadening in their application and a tendency to use a larger, sometimes much larger, format. It was however his subject matter which signalled that he was troubled. In a very beautiful picture, *Greedies Threatening a Peaceful Village* (pl. 24), the baleful and savage faces of the enemy hover and peer from above and behind the roofs, but a little later they have taken over the village. They are it.

It is however a series of totems, largely on black backgrounds and much larger than anything he had done before, which indicates that Scottie was on the edge of a breakdown (pls. 27–34). In these the effect, for the first time since the early 'doodling' period, is psychotic, closer to the drawings of confined 'outsiders'. They are magnificent but profoundly disturbing. Much later, in an interview with Edwin Mullins in *The Weekend Telegraph*, Scottie described how these faces materialized: 'I used to see faces dissolving like someone had poured tar over them, or rather like snowmen melting away.' For some time though, towards the end of the Forties, the faces neither dissolved nor melted. They watched.

Scottie's own 'clown face' with the big droopy nose is often included in these pictures in a state of fear or apprehension, and usually hemmed in or sandwiched between the phantasmagoria. Some of them have horns or expose purposeful teeth. Many metamorphose into carnivorous-looking, monstrous birds and Bosch-like hybrids. Frequently these faces are bound together by coarse intertwined ribbons resembling seaweed. For all those who think of Scottie, usually on the basis of his later and more familiar work, as whimsical or merely decorative, these pictures are a stern corrective. They may lack the delicate poetry and shimmering colour of his Canadian and early British images but they are, in my view, the climax, however sombre and disturbing, of his truly creative years. There was much charm and delight to come but it is marred by repetition and increasing sweetness. It is as though, for some reason, both his angels and demons deserted him. Only towards the very end of his life was he to become aware again of their disquieting presence.

7

'Nowadays my birds are more tender'

'But nowadays my birds are more tender. My earlier birds were bigger – fiercer' said Scottie to Mervyn Levy in an interview for *Studio* (June 1962). After the departure of the 'Greedies' and the 'Evils', Scottie's lightening of the spirit imposed a new technique. Whereas before he had drawn and hatched exclusively in black ink, he now began to use a variety of coloured inks, black amongst them certainly, but also pink, blue, green, and yellows, sometimes but by no means always, reinforced by coloured crayons. At the same time he frequently devised a series of wave-like friezes crossing the picture: swans in one wave, fish in another, flowers in a third, a facade of houses in a fourth. Sometimes too he would enclose such imagery in a rectangular frame containing isolated plants or animals, or box in his creatures within the picture itself, especially so in the case of his fish, which are frequently confined to a bowl-shaped circle.

To begin with, an occasional marauding 'Greedy' or a small band of 'Evils' would put in an appearance, but faced by an increasingly tranquil world, they soon retreated. Often above this idyllic landscape there floated, sun-like, his 'clown' self-portrait shown as always in full-face, but now rather more wistful than tragic in expression, and sometimes crowned with a village or castle, an image which always reminds me of Magritte's *Le Château des Pyrénées* (*overleaf*), in which a huge rock, also capped by a castle, floats above the sea. (Although Magritte was one of the few painters for whom Scottie expressed admiration this resemblance is pure coincidence. Magritte's picture was not conceived until 1959.)

Much of the imagery of this period is interesting and inventive, but the overall impression is weaker and more decorative than anything which preceded it. The use of coloured inks tends to produce a rather sentimental and wishy-washy effect, and there are signs too of a proliferation of almost identical images for purely decorative ends. Whereas in early Scottie one felt that each picture was a unique creation, there is increasingly the feeling that the artist is beginning to think in series. The tension is evaporating.

Scottie's life had, by this time, become more or less settled; the room in Kilburn, the visits to his gallery, the private views; but he did, very occasionally, go abroad in pursuit of his interests. In 1952 for example, he

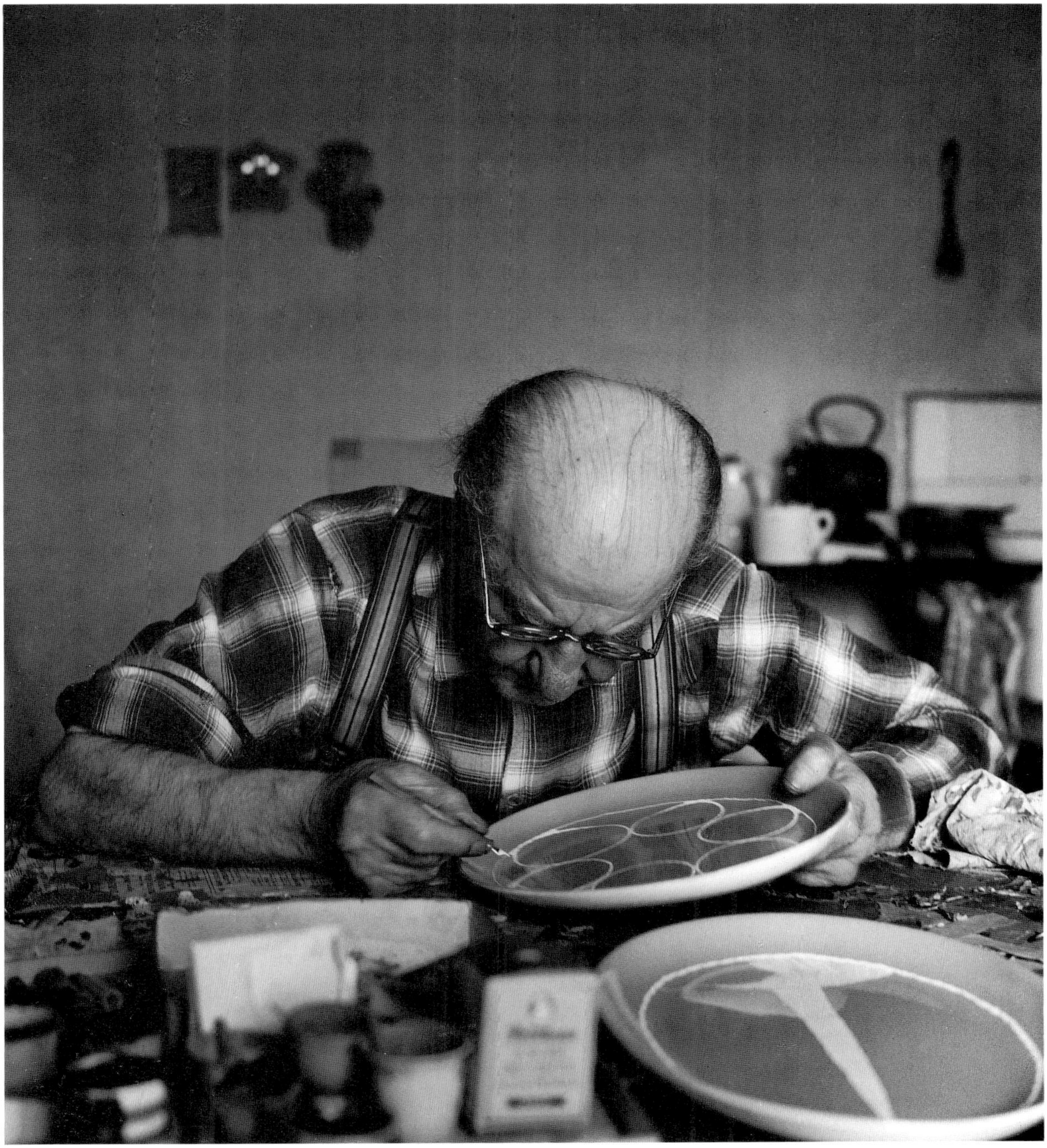

Scottie painting a plate in his room in Kilburn, *c.* 1965. Photo: Ida Kar

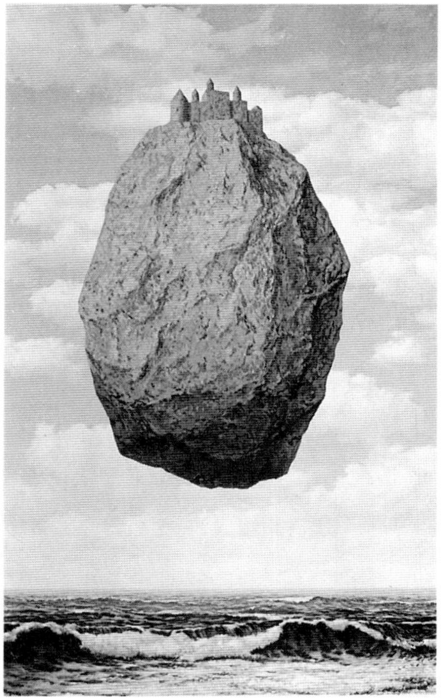

Le Château des Pyrénées by René Magritte, 1959. (Israel Musem, Jerusalem; the gift of Harry Torczyner.) Compare with plate 41

went to Paris mostly to see Dubuffet, the painter and entrepreneur of L'Art Brut who was acquiring a considerable collection of his work. As he spoke no French and, despite his army career, was of a rather insular turn of mind, it might seem a somewhat foolhardy and courageous venture on Scottie's part, but as always he made quite certain that he was looked after. In Old Compton Street, Soho, there was then a small cafe called The French, the haunt of a number of Soho lay-abouts and liggers of Bohemian temperament. The attraction of The French, which was otherwise both dirty and gloomy, lay in the proprietor's tolerance as to the length of time his customers could linger over a single cup of tea. It was also warm, and Scottie went there quite often when 'up West'. One afternoon he overheard Bill Hopkins (see above, p. 16) announce that he intended to visit Paris for a fortnight. Scottie asked him if he could accompany him, and Hopkins, with a certain reluctance, agreed.
appointed day, Scottie wearing, according to Hopkins, a threadbare pin-

From then on, until his departure, Scottie clung to Hopkins like a leech for fear he should leave without him. They set off together on the appointed day, Scottie wearing, according to Hopkins, a threadbare pinstriped suit and a bowler hat in place of his usual cap. He carried, amongst his few possessions, his painting materials, some completed works, and a list of those he wished to contact. Hopkins remembers the visit with qualified enthusiasm. His intention was to meet up with various literary figures, but he found himself, more often than not, acting as Scottie's interpreter and guide. They shared a room near the Panthéon and Scottie would sit up late into the night, working, delivering monologues and occasionally laughing to himself at the exact moment when Hopkins was on the point of dropping off. He complained a great deal about the food, appeared entirely indifferent to his surroundings, and constantly expressed his longing to return to London.

There was however, for Hopkins, the recompense of the visit to Dubuffet. The painter received Scottie with enthusiastic admiration which was, as usual, taken as no more than his due. Dubuffet also purchased several recent works and then, just as they were about to leave, Picasso arrived. At first, failing to hear the introductions, Picasso ignored the rather odd bowler-hatted little figure, and spent his time shuffling rapidly through Dubuffet's work stacked against the walls of the studio, but then, when his attention was drawn to Scottie's pictures, Picasso, realizing who he was, praised him highly, and told him that he possessed several of his works in his own collection. He left soon afterwards (Dubuffet complaining that the purpose of the master's visit was to see what ideas might be useful to him) and after a short interval Scottie and Hopkins followed suit. Hopkins was impressed, not only at having met the world's most famous living painter, but also that Scottie, who naturally enough was well aware of Picasso, showed no interest either in the painter himself nor in the fact that he owned his work.

Later on Scottie was to pay several visits to Switzerland where he had a number of serious collectors. Eventually he was commissioned to design a large mural for a bank in Zürich, and was flown over for a lunch for the unveiling. It was of course ironic that Scottie, with his anarchistic principles, should have been chosen to embellish one of the symbols of capitalism and it was perhaps fortunate that by this time the 'Greedies' had given way to innocuous little birds, lakes and castles. On his return he complained to the Gimpels, who were at that time his dealers, 'There were the bankers', he said, 'with all their bags of gold, and me sitting there without the price of a kipper in me pocket.' It's a splendidly cartoon-like image although, as presumably the gold-laden bankers had opened their bags to pay Scottie for his work, not entirely factual.

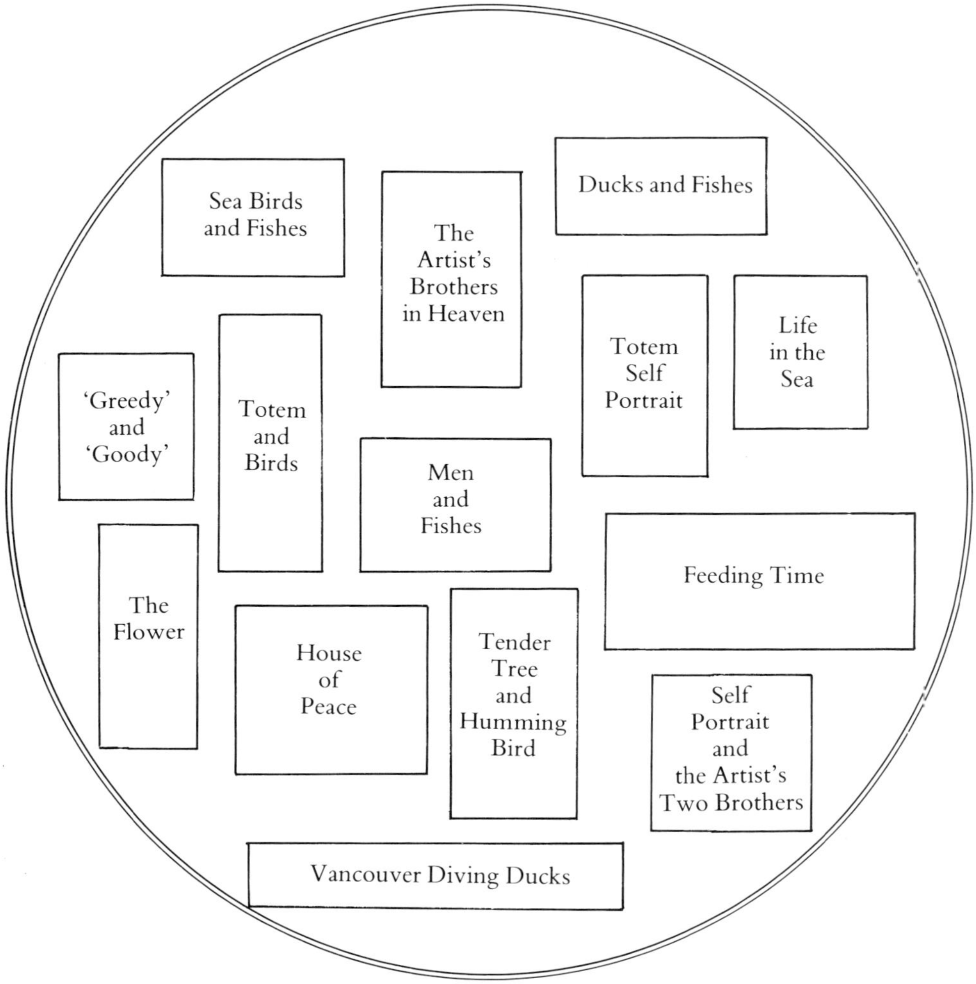

The painting reproduced opposite is a self portrait of Scottie Wilson as a pierrot or clown holding in his hands the world, which is filled with fourteen of his most famous picture themes. These are explained in the diagram above. The painting is based on an open booth exhibition held by Scottie on Blackpool Front

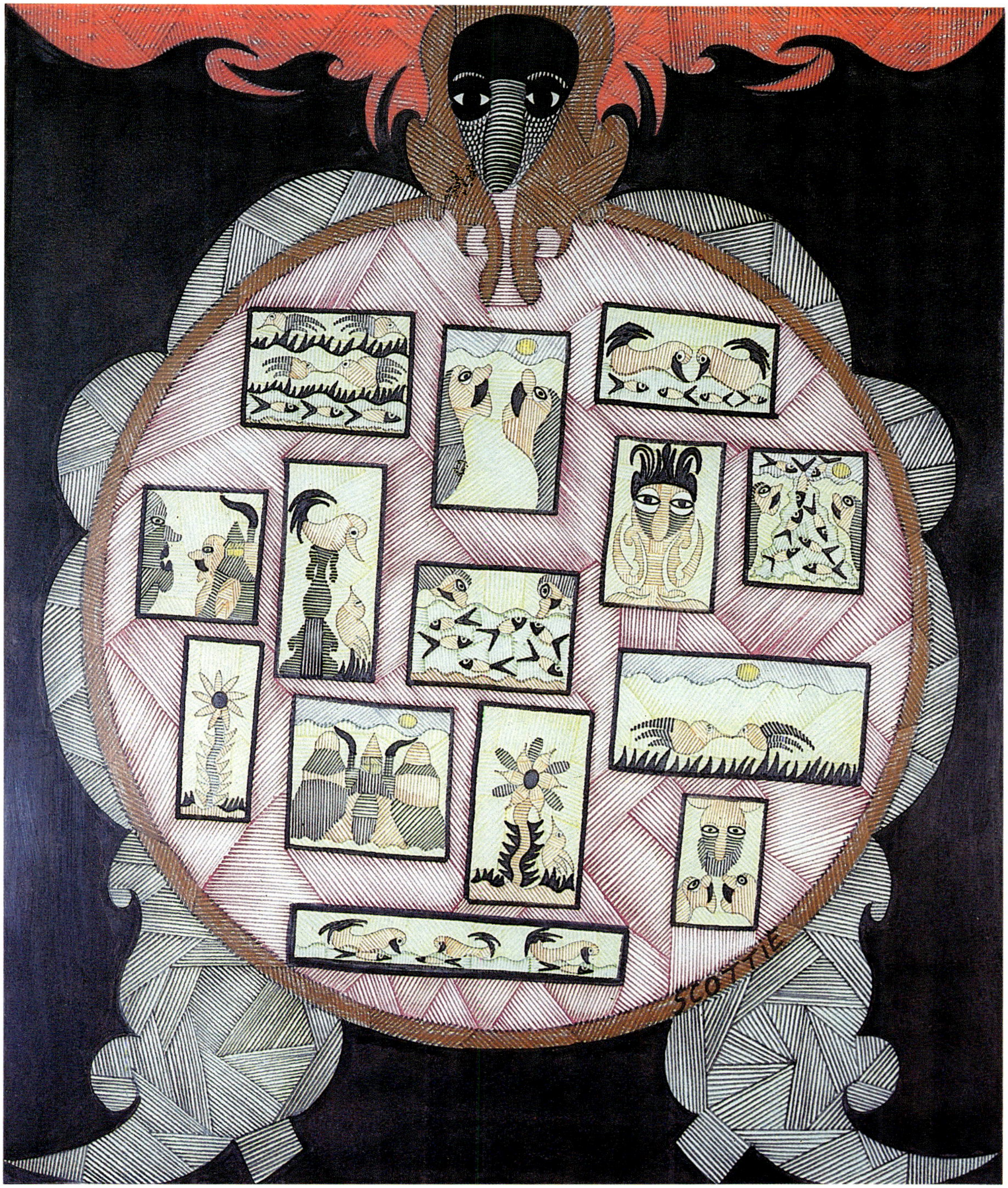

36 *Scottie's Art Gallery*, *c.* 1960. 40.6×40.0. Robert Lewin

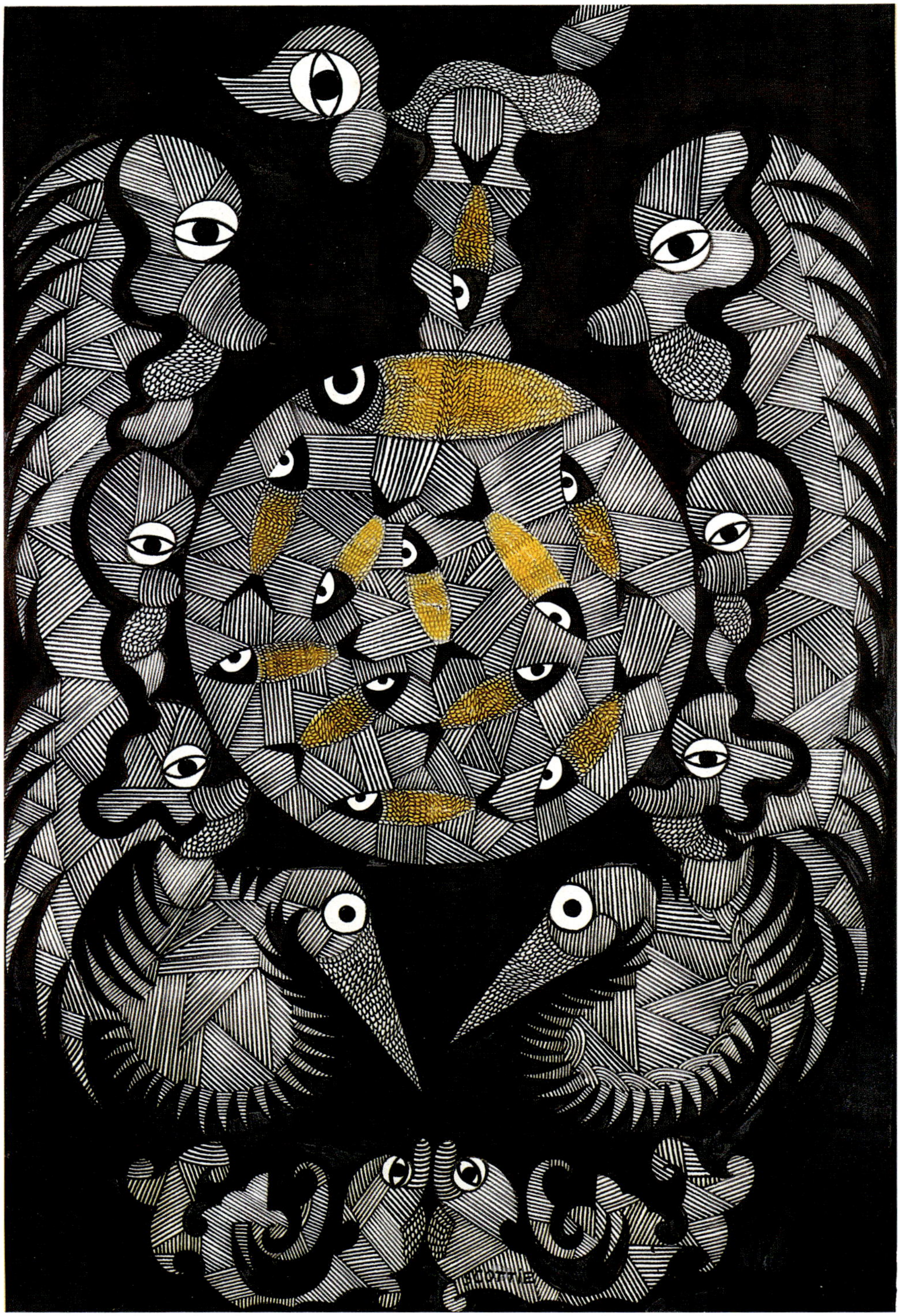

37 *The Seekers*, early 1950s. 49.0×35.5. Gimpel Fils Gallery, London

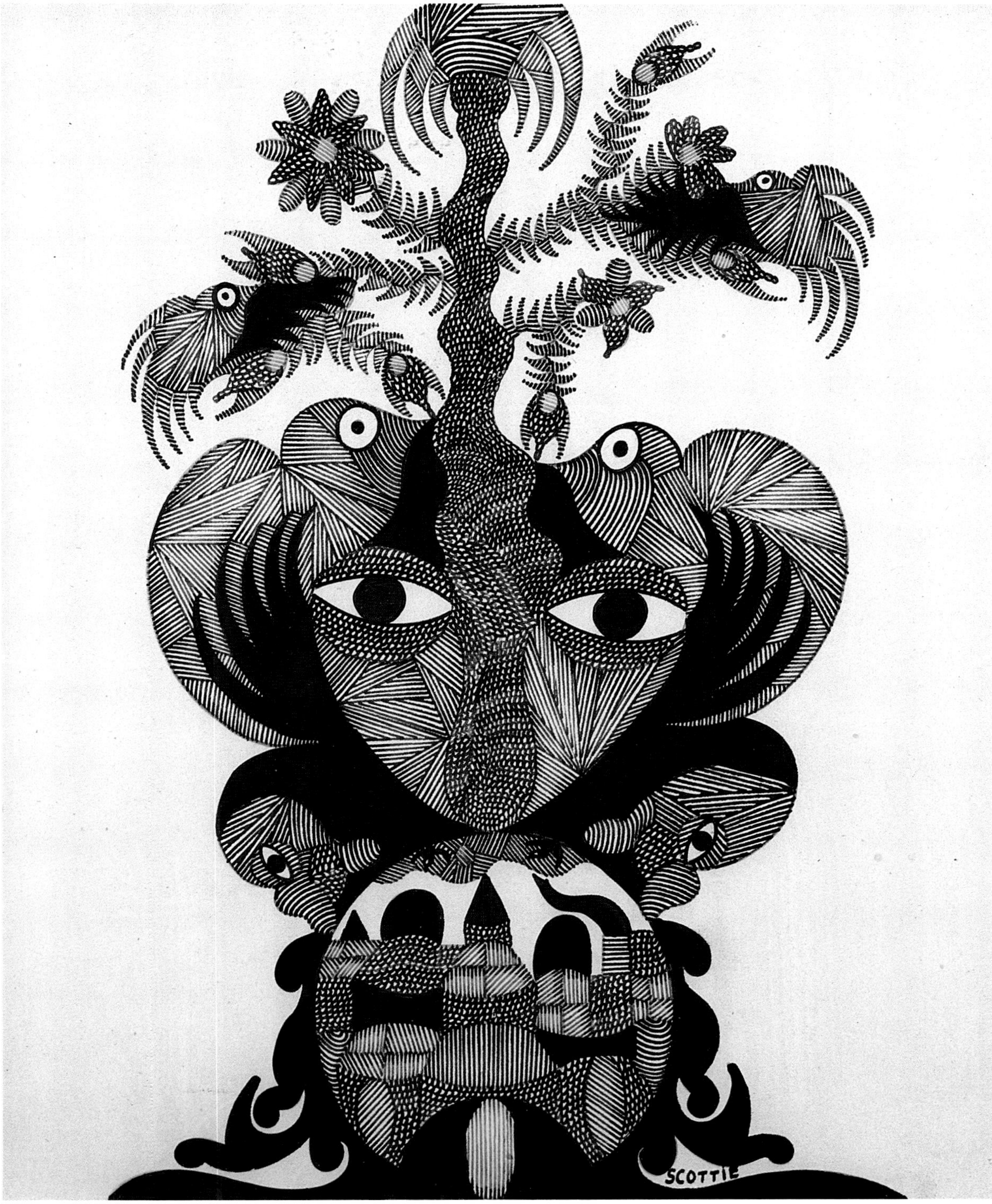

38 *Self Portrait with Birds*, *c.* 1950. 31.0×26.0. Gimpel Fils Gallery, London

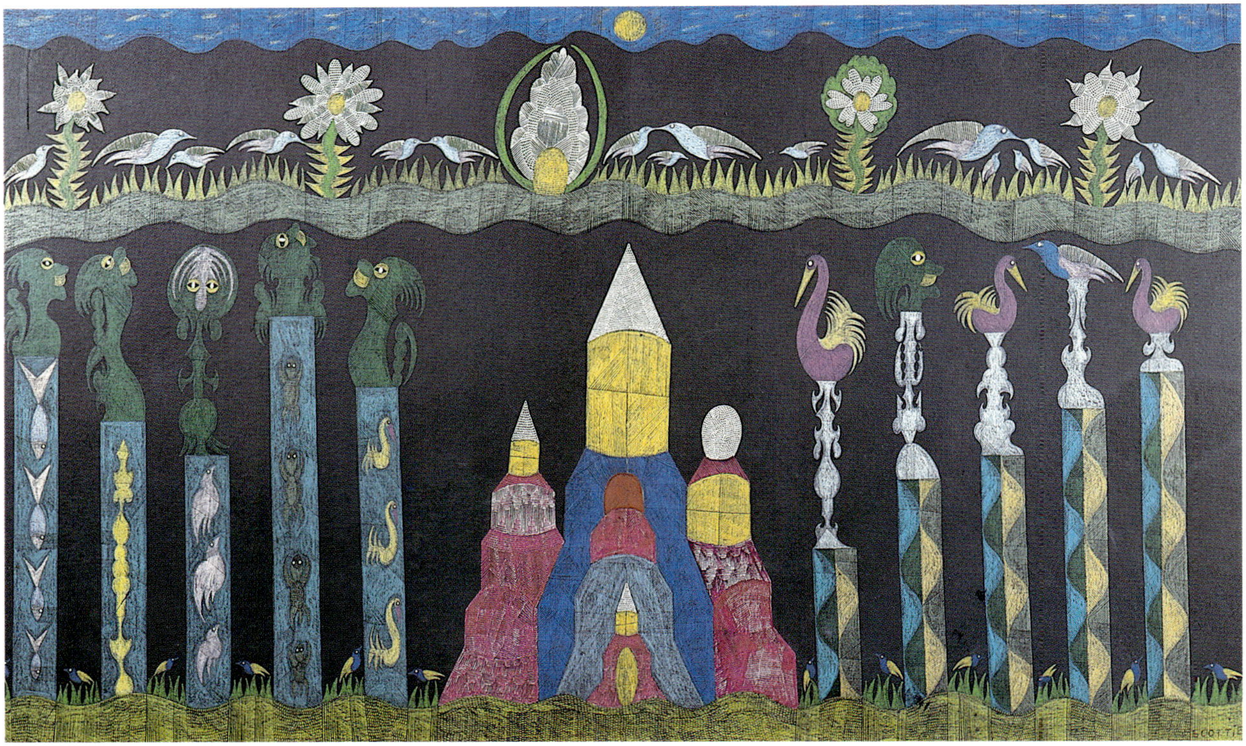

39 *Whispering Paradise*, 1951. 90.2×152.4. Scottish National Gallery of Modern Art, Edinburgh

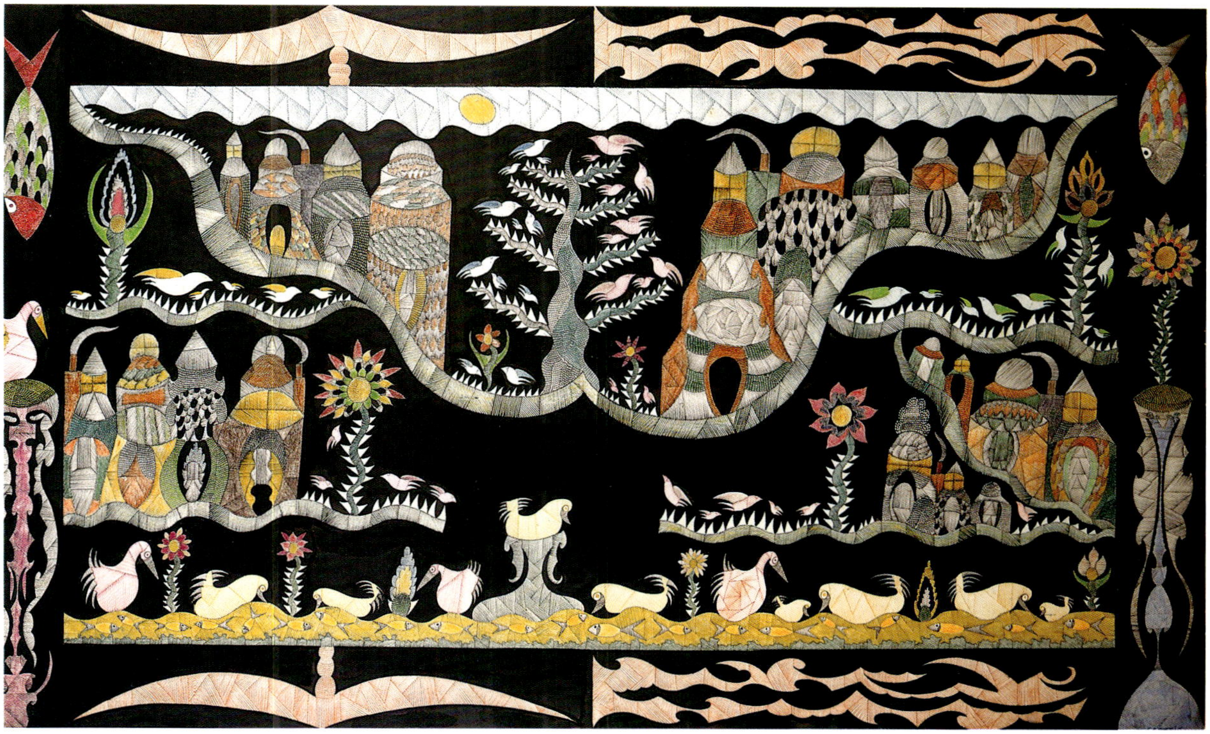

40 *Springtime*, 1952. 89.0×148.5. Gimpel Fils Gallery, London

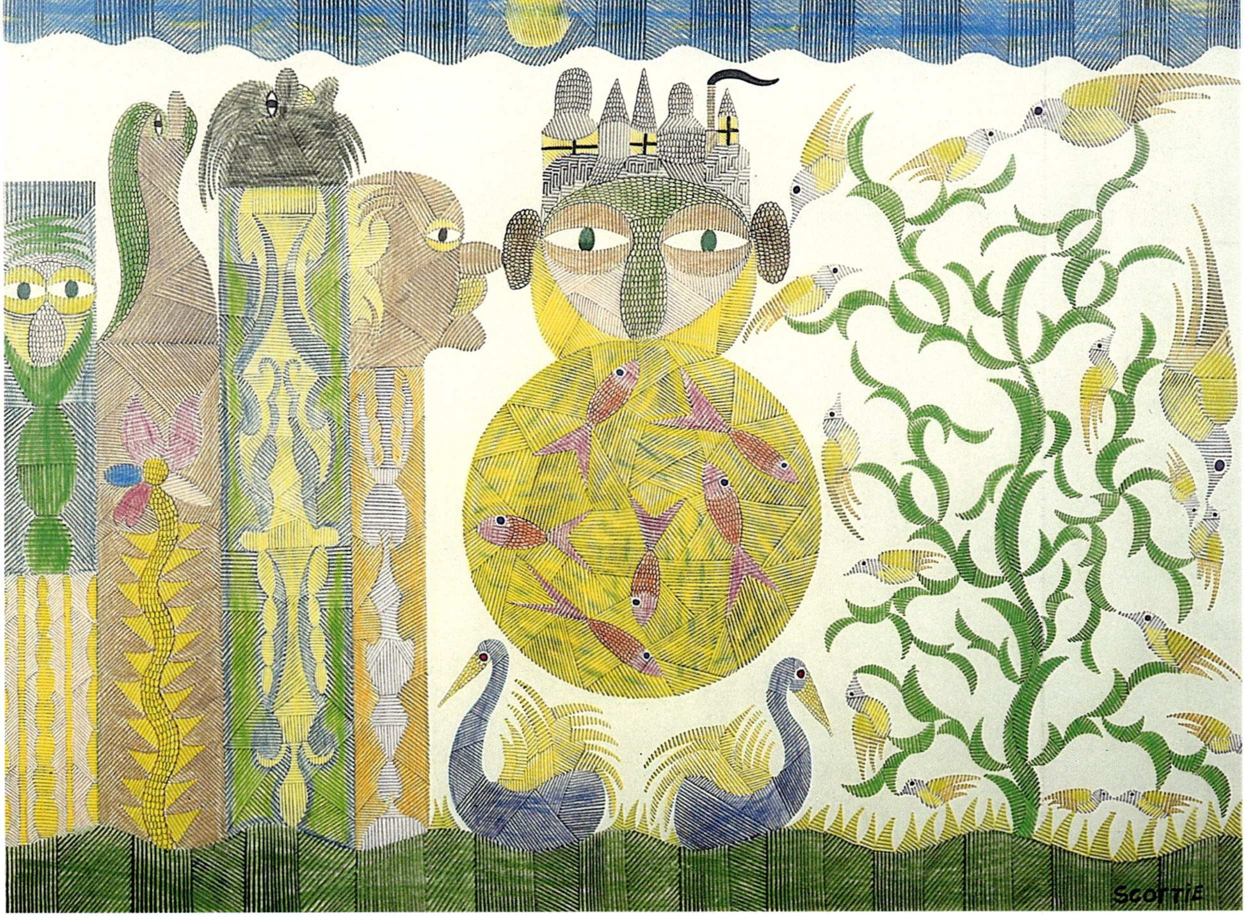

41 Untitled, *c.* 1950. 38.1×58.4. Robert Lewin

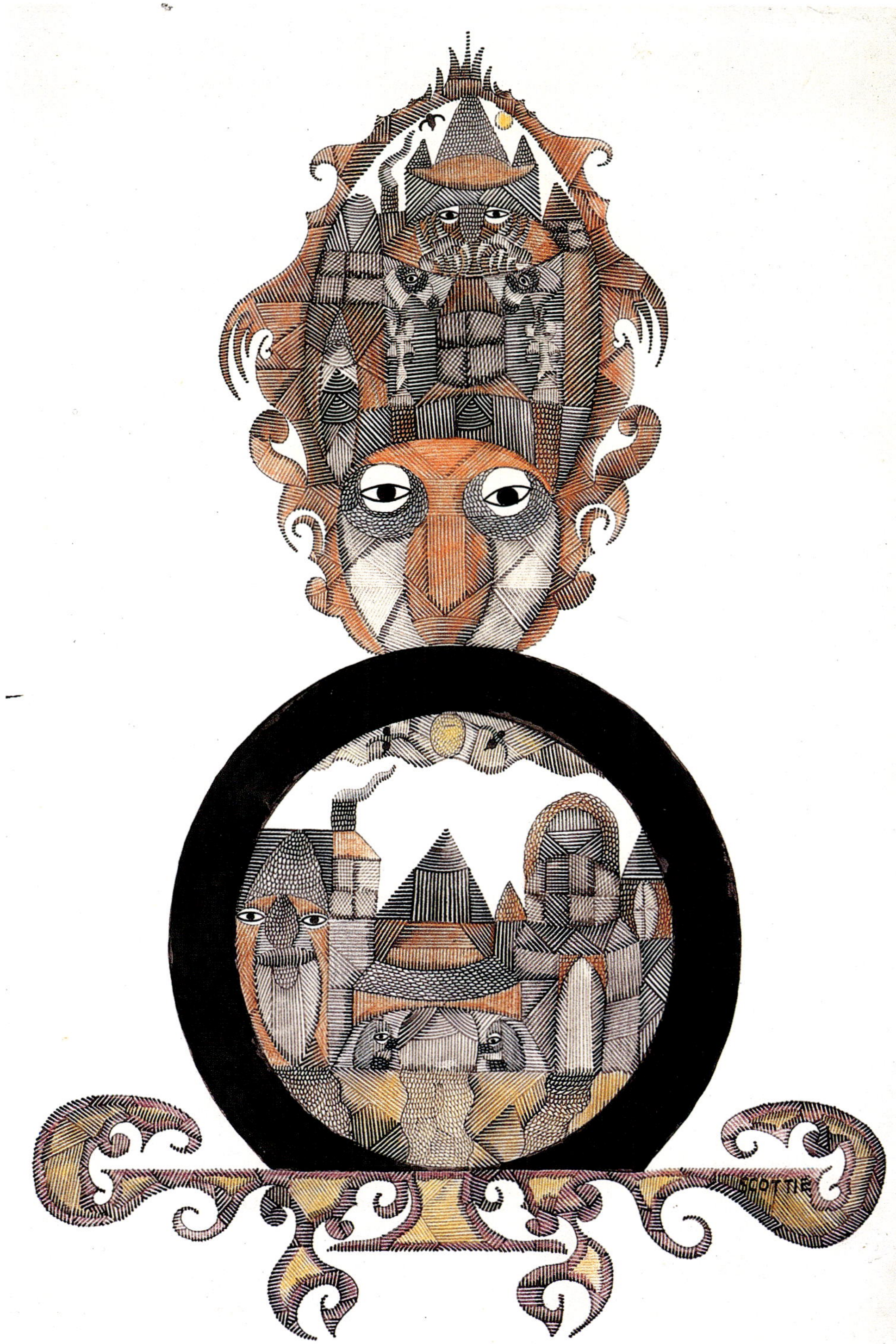

42 *Thinking about Houses*, 1950. 57.0×38.0. Collection de L'Art Brut, Lausanne

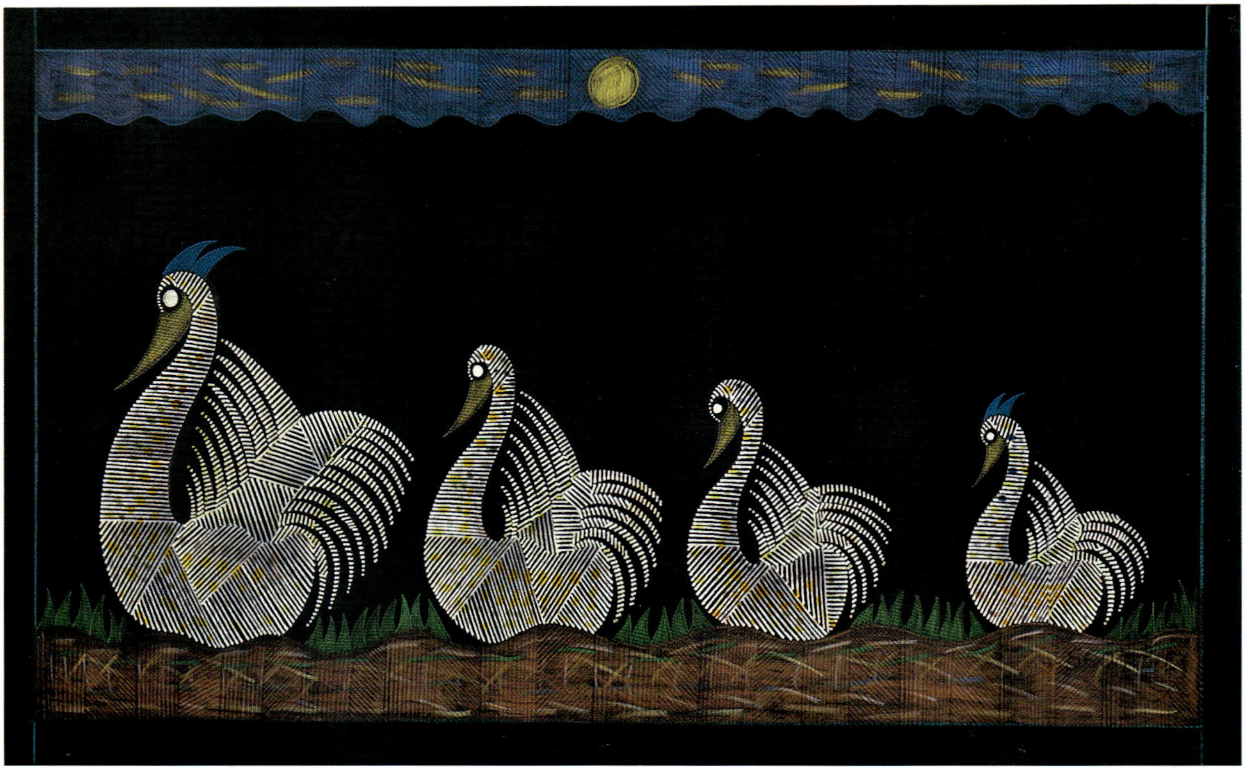

43 Untitled, *c.* 1960. 28.6×50.8. Robert Lewin

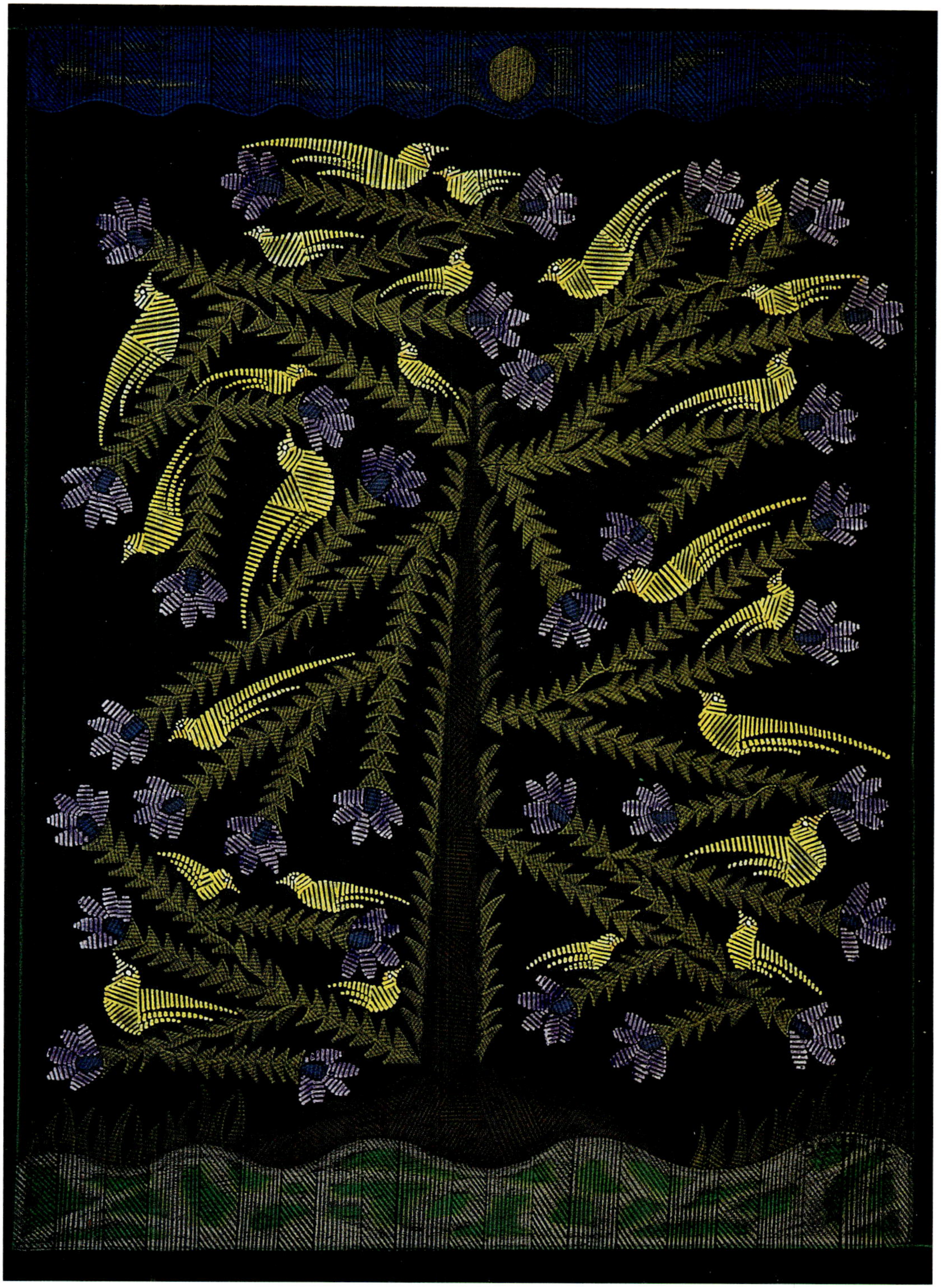

44 Untitled, *c.* 1960. 52.0×39.0. Private collection

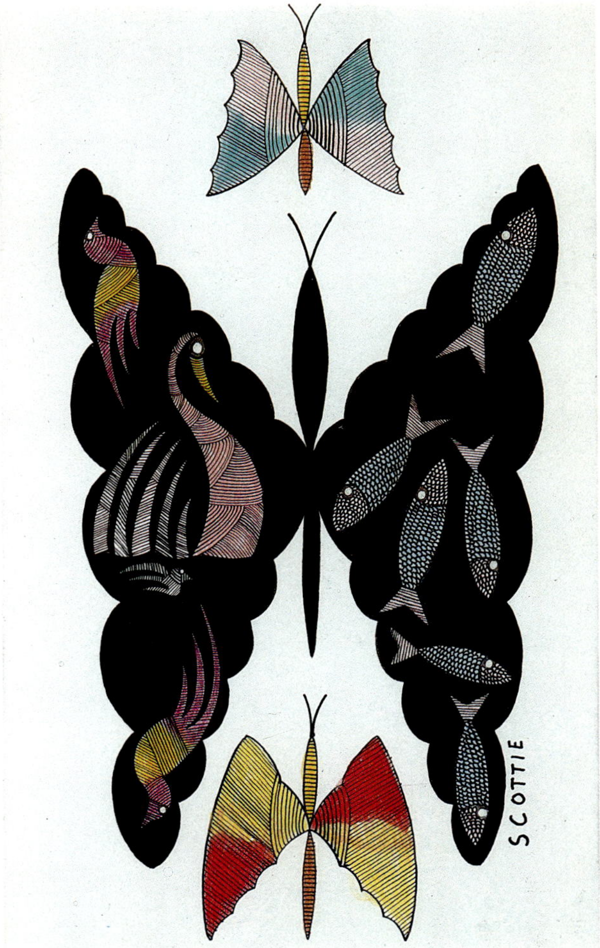

45 *Swan's Butterfly*, *c.* 1970. 38.1×24.8.
Mercury Gallery, London

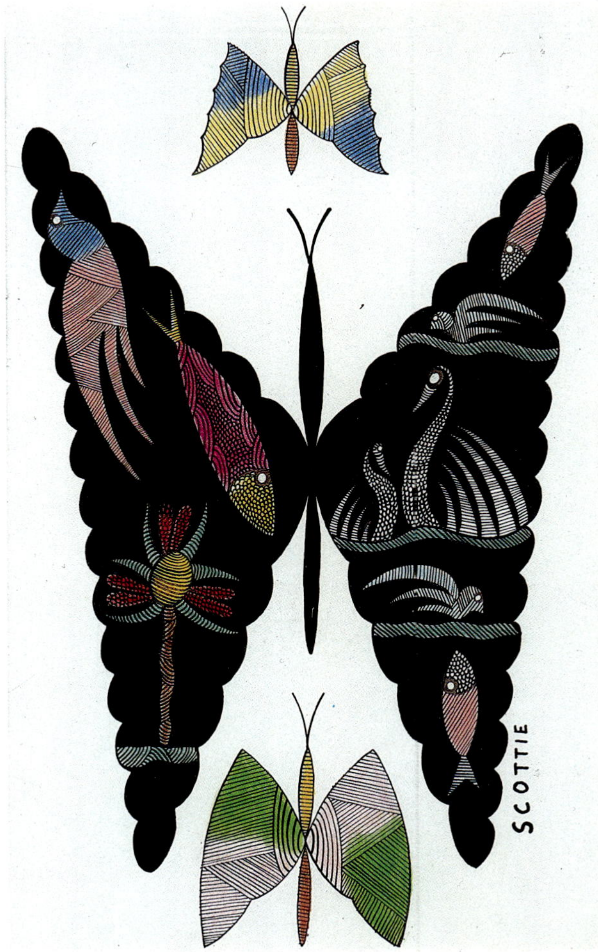

46 *Butterfly*, *c.* 1970. 38.1×24.8.
Mercury Gallery, London

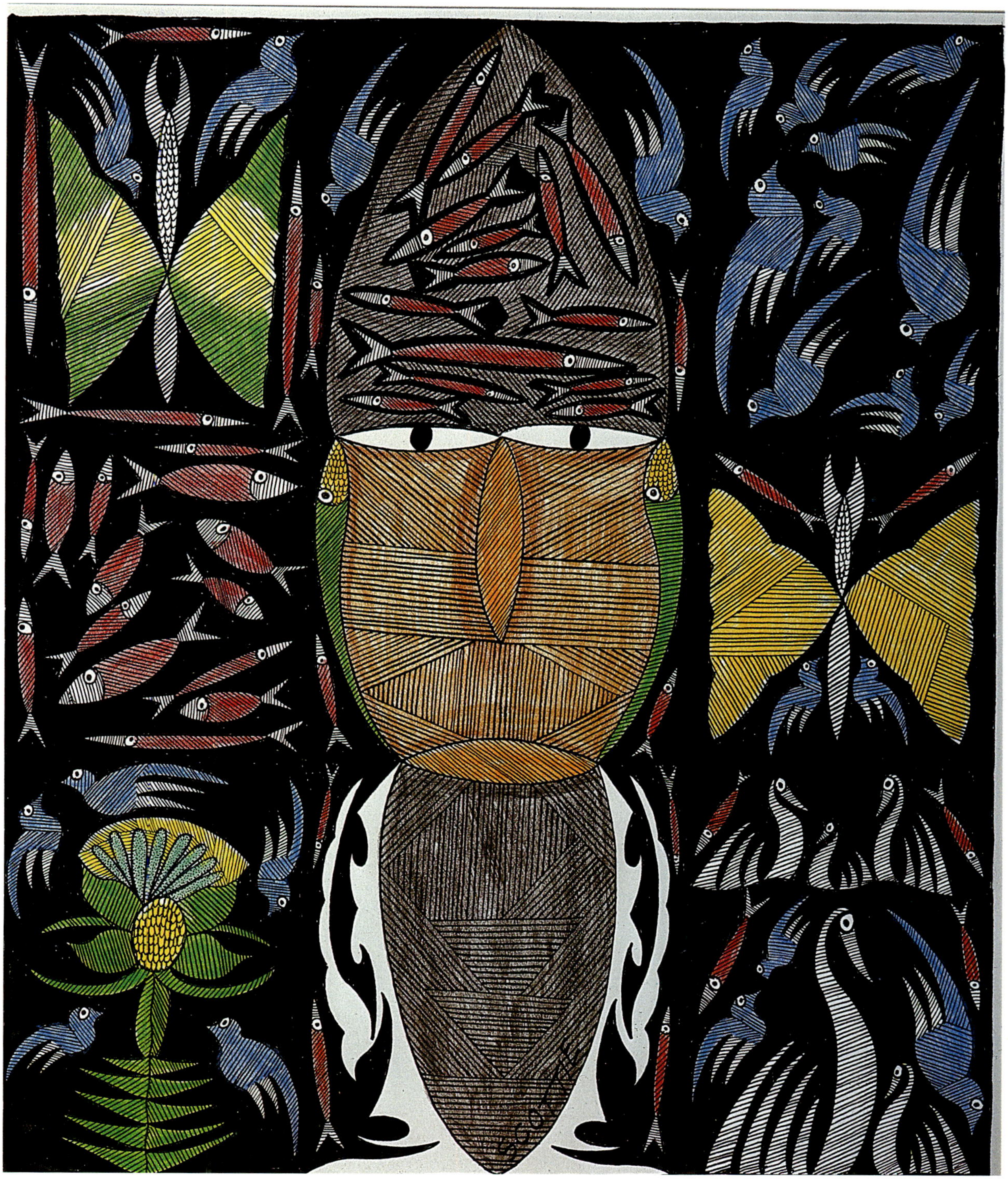

47 Untitled, *c.* 1970. 35.6×30.5. Robert Lewin

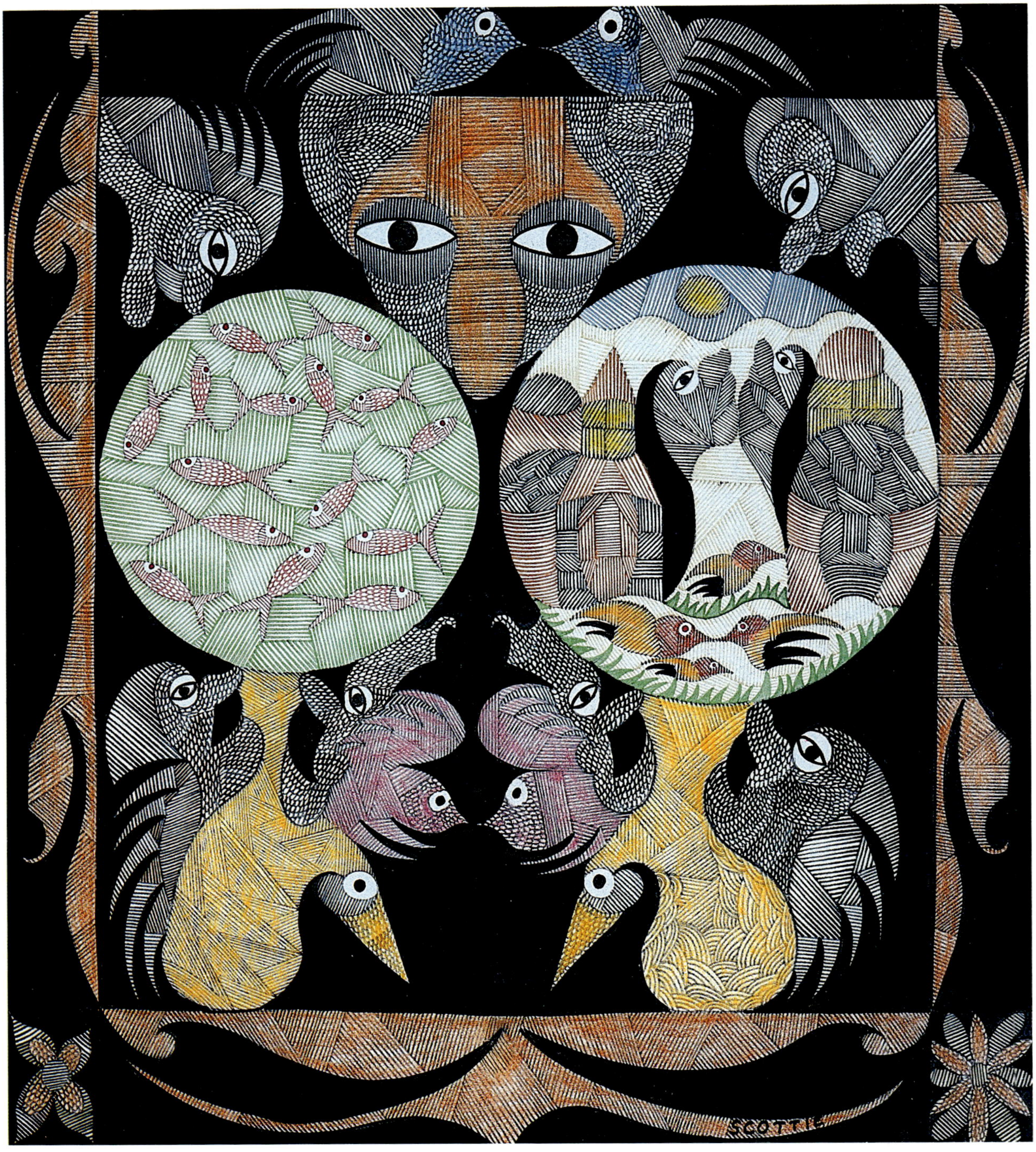

48 *Crystal Gazers*, 1950–1. 43.0×38.5. Collection de L'Art Brut, Lausanne

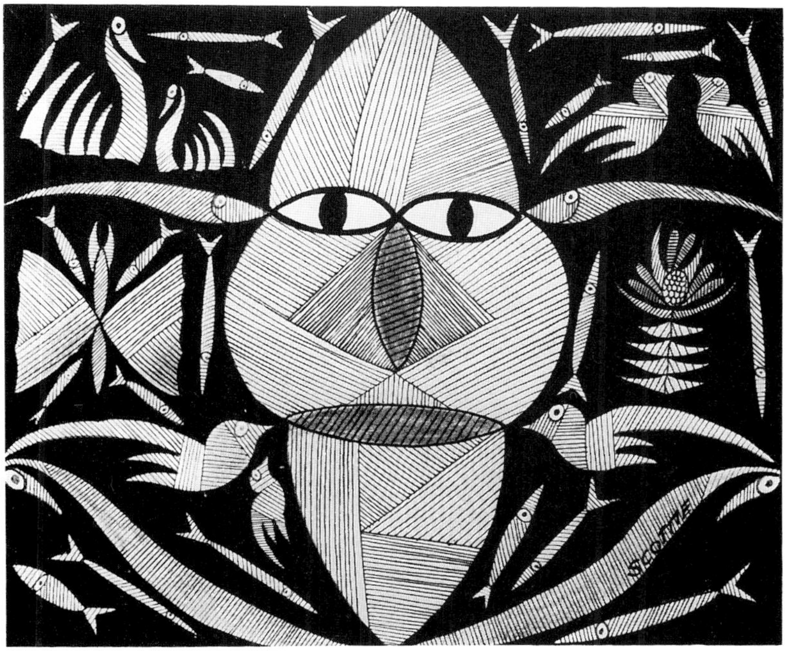

Above: Untitled, late 1960s. Dimensions unknown. Carl Laszlo.
Below: Untitled, late 1960s. Dimensions unknown. Carl Laszlo

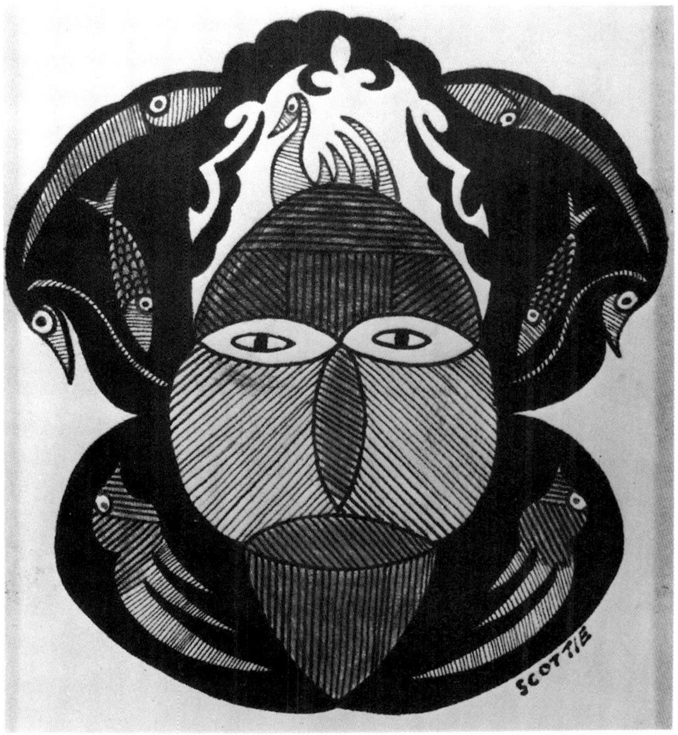

Around the beginning of the Sixties, Scottie extended his technique yet again by gradually introducing flat washes of bright colour alternating with the pen strokes in coloured ink. Simultaneously he was reducing his imagery, confining it entirely to swans, with increasingly ornate tails, small birds frequently present in large quantities perching along the branches of a formalized tree, fish, huge flowers, water, castles and small houses (pls. 43–44). Often these images were framed by decorative mounts giving them something of the look of an Eastern carpet. Human faces, whether benevolent or menacing, entirely vanished from his work.

Compared with the invention and driven quality of his earlier work, I find most of these pictures, and they exist in huge quantities, of very little interest. They are undeniably decorative and they charm, but that is all. They were however far more popular with the public than was his earlier work, and it is significant that a Scottie design was printed on an Ascher scarf. During the same period he began to paint on plates which he then varnished. These stimulated the interest of Robert Baker, late Professor of Ceramics at the Royal College of Art, and then Art Director of the Royal Worcester Porcelain Company, and in 1965 he commissioned Scottie to design dinner, tea and coffee services (see Mervyn Levy's book). It was all a long way from the 'bulldog' pen in the back-room of a Toronto junk shop.

It is always wrong to blame an artist for achieving a certain happiness even if, as in this case, it weakens his work. The later pictures are touching, even idyllic, but if they were all we knew, I suspect that Scottie Wilson would be considered as no more than a quaint naive. As it is, because they are not the whole story, he is so much more than that.

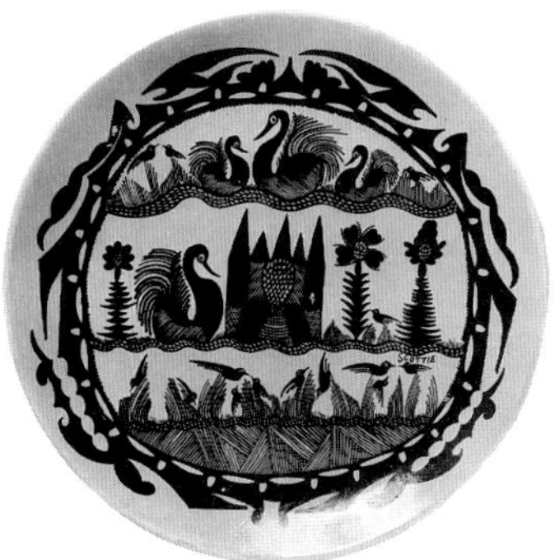

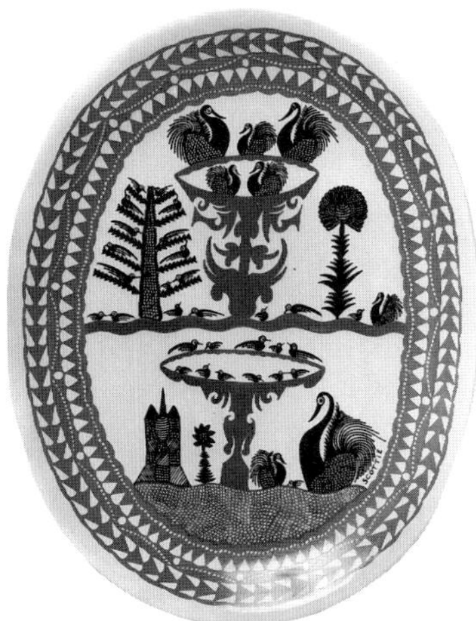

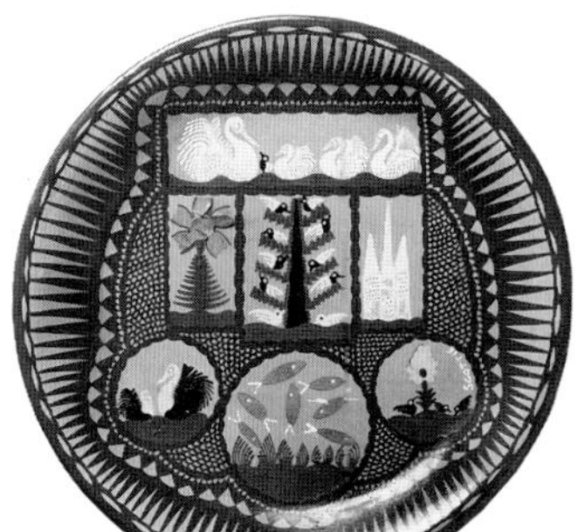

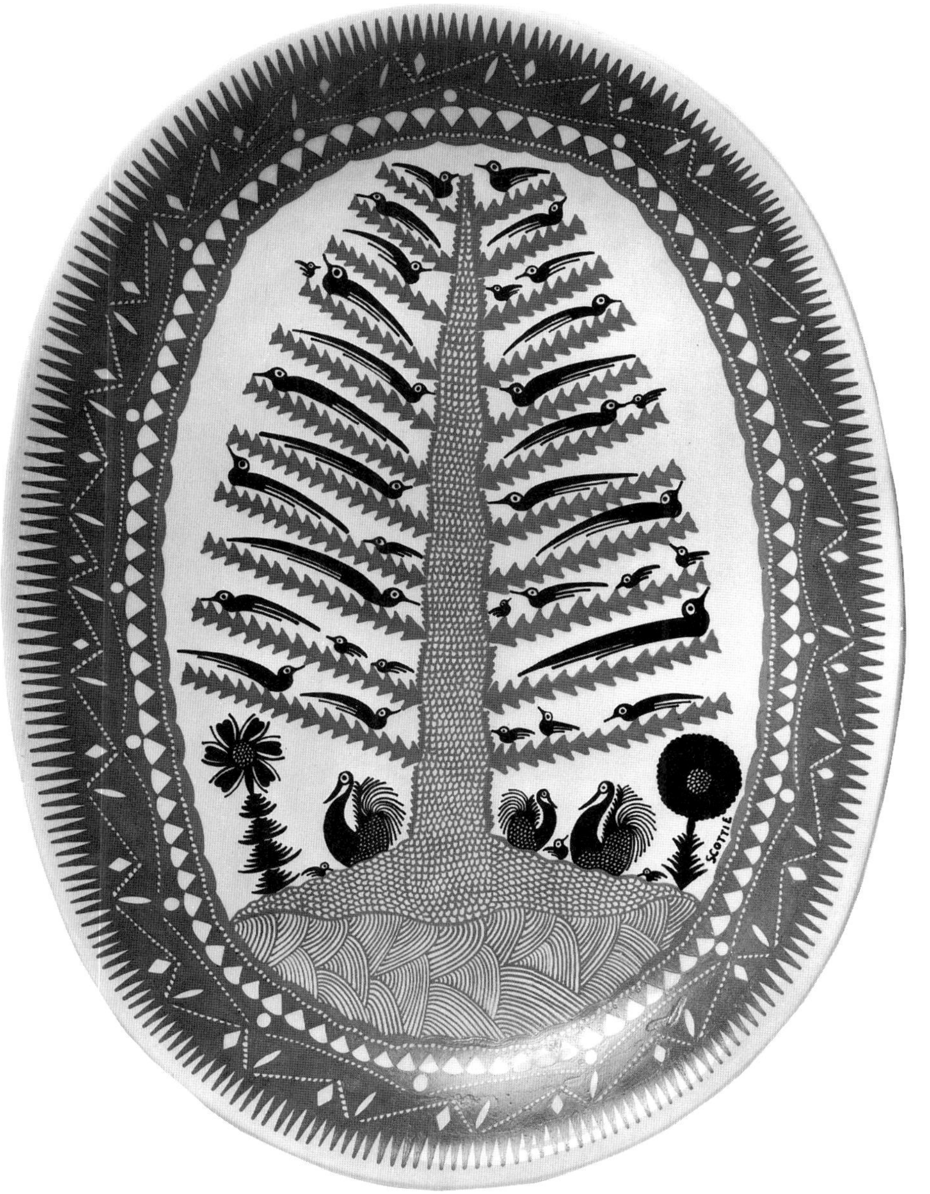

Opposite and above: A selection of Scottie's plates, all painted in the 1960s.
All from private collections

8

'By God – Aye!'

Clifford Myerson was Scottie's doctor from 1962 until Scottie died. He used to visit him regularly, not that there was much wrong with him until the very end but because Dr Myerson felt that, while increasingly a recluse, Scottie needed someone to talk to. Realizing that Scottie was obsessional about routine, Myerson always arrived at the same time and on the same day. Scottie would become angry if for some reason he was unable to come.

Dr Myerson got the impression that he was Scottie's only regular visitor, but now realizes that this was not the case. There were also Mervyn Levy and his wife and probably others. Scottie was very secretive. There was, for example, a painting of a boat on the wall. When questioned, Scottie told him that it was by a painter from Essex and he thought it 'very neat'. Myerson thought Scottie was touchy but very intelligent, and, had he been able to read and write, could have achieved anything. He might have become – like Peter Cook's park-bench derelict who 'hadn't got the Latin' – a judge. He couldn't however explain his pictures.

Scottie once asked Myerson why people didn't come and see him 'Perhaps', said his friend, 'they're frightened you might hit them.' (There had been a rumour that Scottie had hit somebody in a pub.) Scottie countered this suggestion by maintaining that 'A man who paints little birds on trees doesn't hit people.' Scottie's relationship with Mervyn Levy was more turbulent. Apparently he was always including or excluding him from his will.

In his late seventies, Scottie had an operation for a hernia and removal of his prostate. It was entirely successful from a medical point of view but, being institutionalized and subjected to an imposed routine affected him mentally. He became even more suspicious, even more of a recluse according to Myerson. Gradually the 'Evils' and the 'Greedies' returned, the totem-poles loomed up again, and there was a new image – the butterfly – often thought to herald the approach of death (pls. 45–46).

Scottie's butterflies have no precedents in his work. They are painted in rather crude colours and presented flat against the background as though pinned to a board. Sometimes they appear, much larger than anything

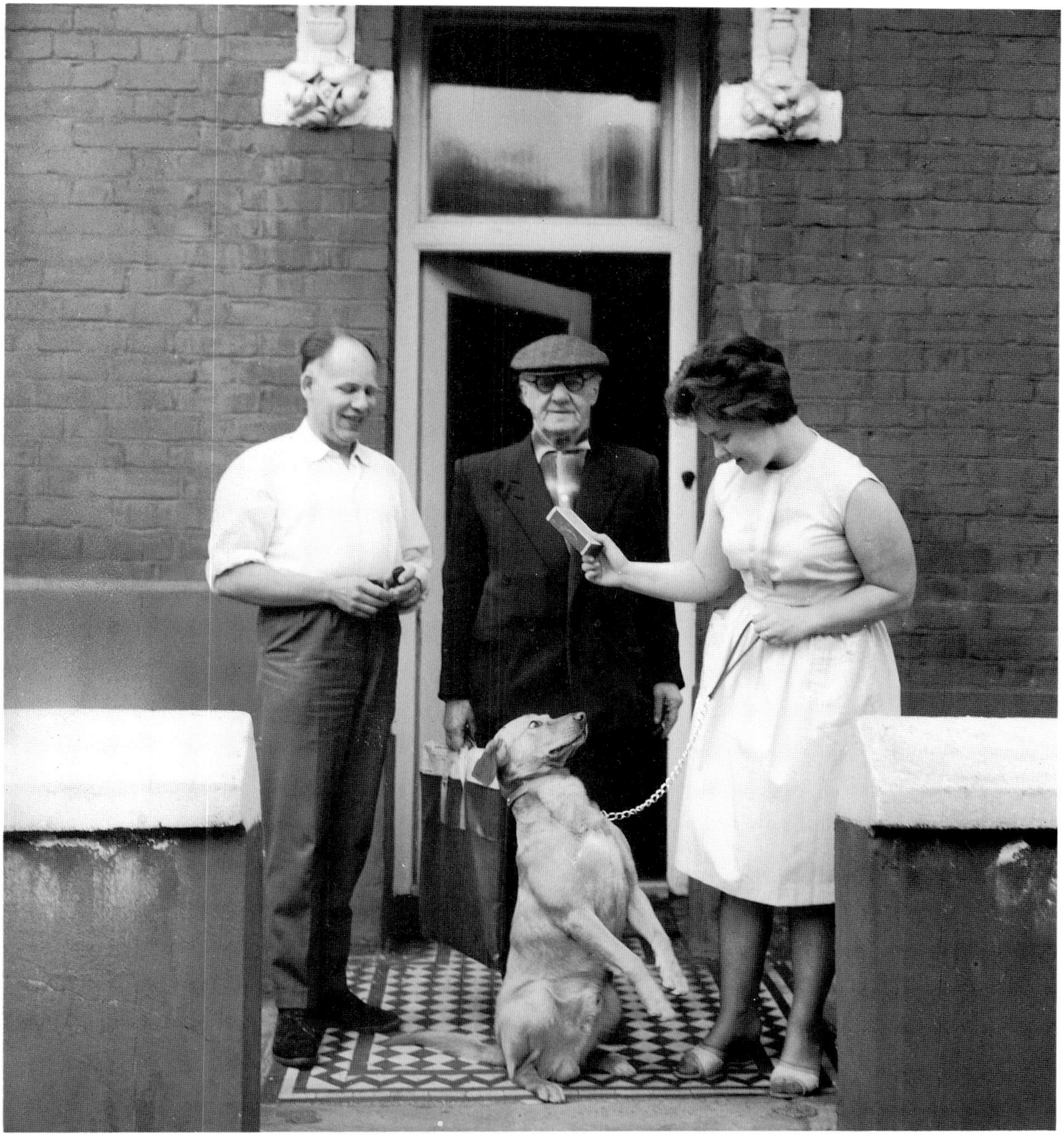

Scottie outside his lodgings in Kilburn, with his landlord and landlady and their dog, *c.* 1965.
Photo Ida Kar

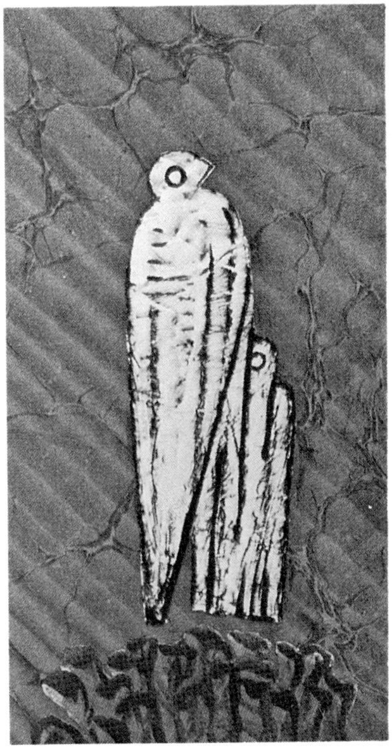

Detail from *Le Facteur Cheval* by Max Ernst, 1932. (Peggy Guggenheim collection, Venice.) Compare with Scottie's birds in the picture reproduced opposite

else, amongst the happy swans and fishes, or containing them within their contours. Sometimes they are the sole subject of a picture, either alone or in evenly separated groupings. Very often, in the butterfly pictures, crawling rather then fluttering across a low horizon are a few highly stylized birds, many of them touching beaks. They have a chilling aspect. There is one late butterfly picture (*opposite*), among his very last works, which is remarkable. A large butterfly, outlined by a wavy white aura is suspended beneath a poached-egg sun with serrated edges and a slice out of it. On the ground two birds touch beaks, another sits alone. It has something of the intensity of a Max Ernst. It is unlike anything else I have seen in Scottie's work.

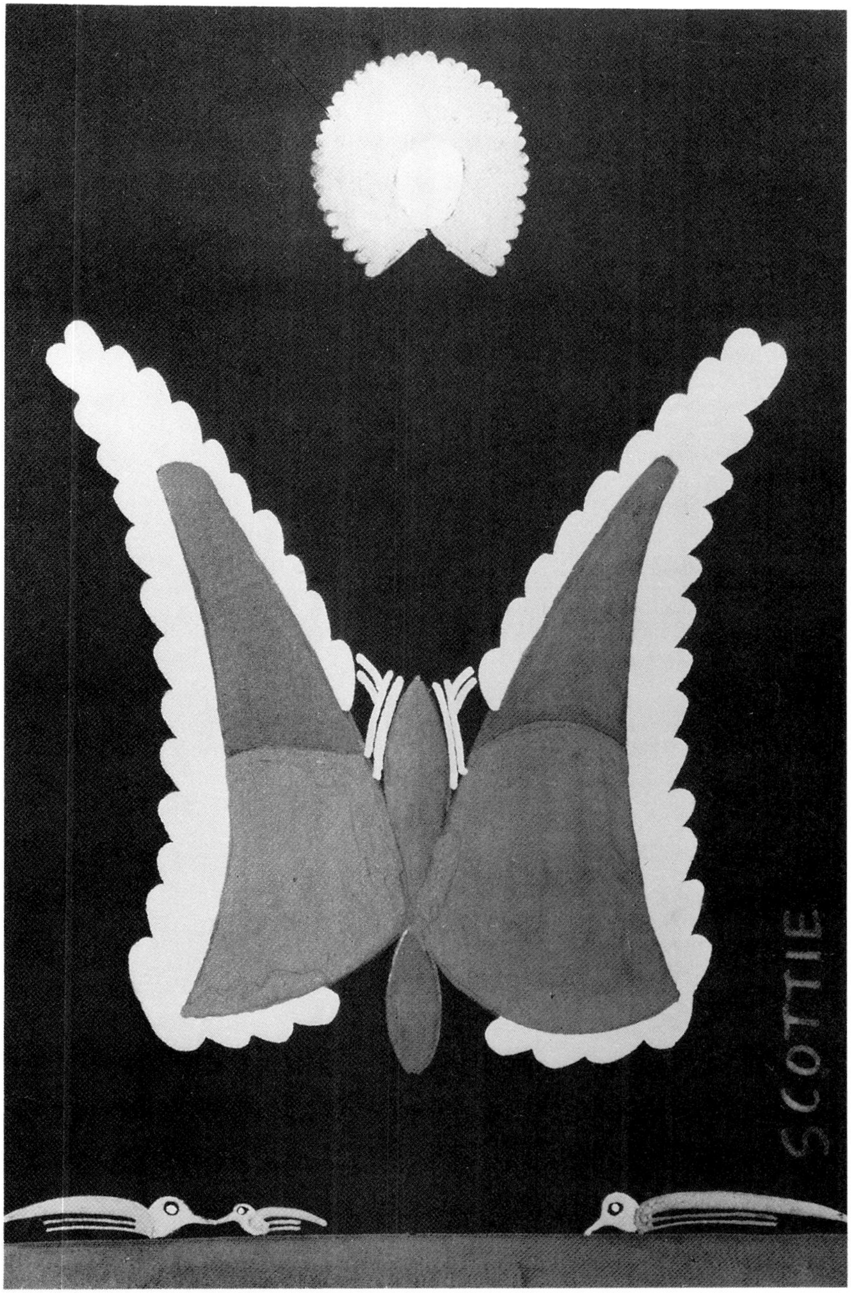

Untitled, 1968. Dimensions and location unknown

In the late faces Scottie returned to hatching with lines. They are much cruder than his early work, but powerful and disturbing. Dr Myerson asked him why these phantoms had returned, and Scottie replied it was because they had returned to him. He saw them.

In his eighties Scottie developed a swollen gland on his neck which turned out to be cancer. He refused to go into hospital for an operation, and, according to Dr Myerson, appeared quite well until only two months before he died, in 1972. He didn't believe he wasn't going to live, fought hard and made plans. At the end he was more or less conscious, responded to what the doctor was doing, and seemed not at all frightened.

Some time before, an income-tax official had approached Dr Myerson to inquire about Scottie's earnings. Myerson explained, having believed Scottie's consistent plea of penury, that he was a poor artist. The official told him that he had made more than he might think. The income-tax official was right, Myerson wrong. After Scottie's death, a suitcase was found under his bed which contained several thousand pounds and there was a comparatively large sum in a bank account. He had, after all, more than the price of a kipper in his pocket.

'Life! – it's all writ out for you – the moves you make . . .'

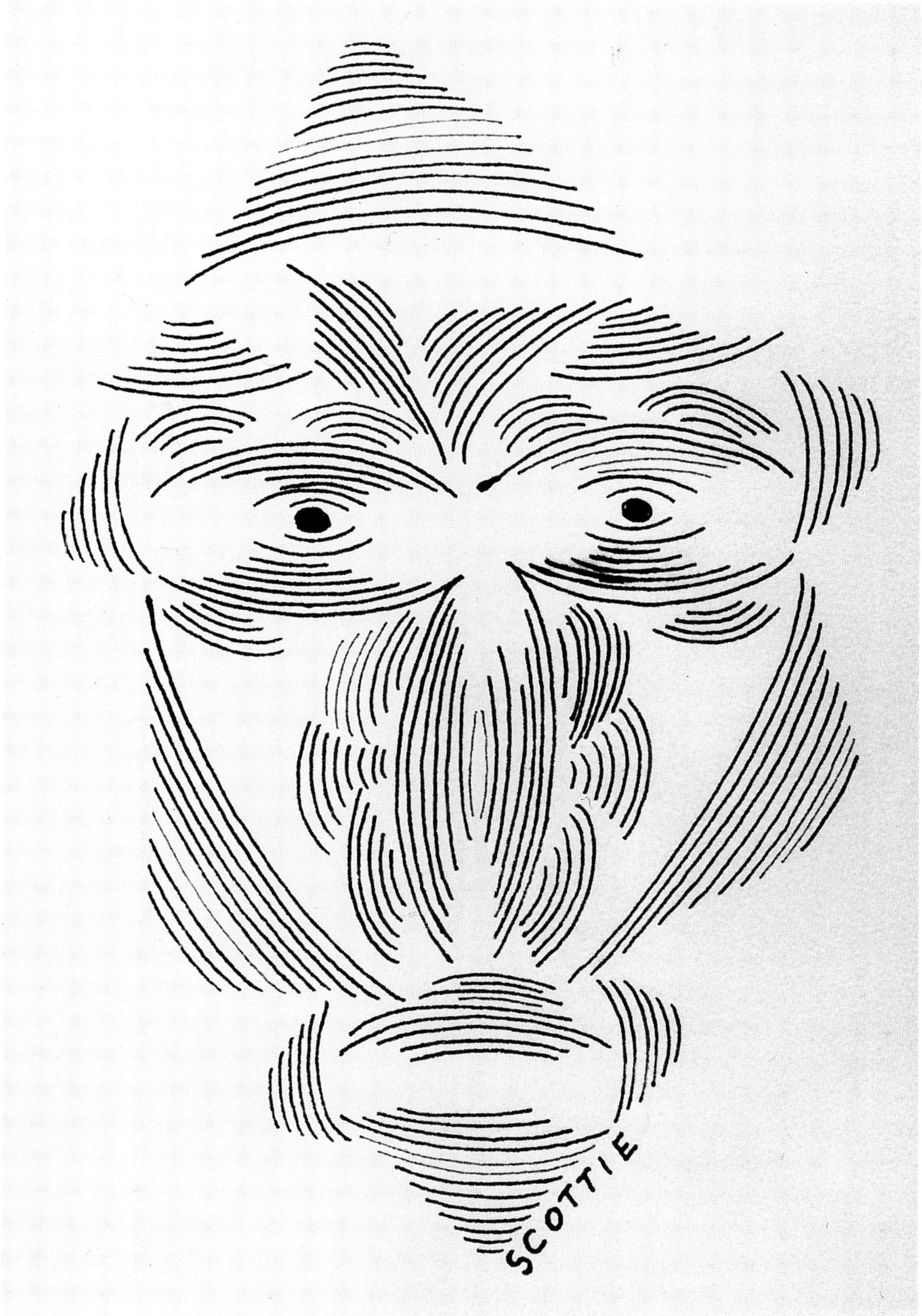

Untitled, *c.* 1970. 20.3×14.0. Professor Bryan Brooke

LIST OF EXHIBITIONS AND COLLECTIONS

One-man exhibitions

1943 Picture Loan Society, Toronto (also exhibitions in Montreal, Winnipeg and Vancouver, *c.* 1943)

1946 'Exhibition of Drawings by Scottie Wilson', Barcelona Restaurant, in association with The London Gallery, London
'350 Works by Scottie Wilson', Newborough, Scarborough

1949 'Pen and Brush by Scottie Wilson', Gimpel Fils Gallery, London
'Exhibition of Decorative Panels', Passediot, New York

1950 'Scottie Wilson', Gimpel Fils Gallery, London

1951 'Scottie Wilson', Gimpel Fils Gallery, London
Galerie Nina Dausset, Paris

1952 Galerie Joos Hutter, Basel
'Scottie Wilson', Gimpel Fils Gallery, London
'The Aubusson Tapestry by Scottie Wilson', Galerie de France, Paris

1962 Ben Uri Gallery, London

1966 'Scottie Wilson', Brook Street Gallery, London

1967 'Scottie Wilson', New Charing Cross Gallery, Glasgow
'Scottie Wilson', Brook Street Gallery, London

1968 'Old and New Images by Scottie Wilson', Circle Paintings, London

1971 'Scottie Wilson, Drawings and Ceramics', Ben Uri Gallery, London

1972 'Scottie Wilson', Fieldbourne Galleries, London

1975 'Scottie Wilson', Margaret Fischer, 2 Lambolle Road, London
'Scottie Wilson', Gimpel Fils Gallery, London

1977 'Scottie Wilson', Warehouse Gallery (Artists' Market), London
'Scottie Wilson', Fieldbourne Galleries, London

1978 'Scottie Wilson', Collection de L'Art Brut, Lausanne

1979 'Scottie Wilson', Galerie Schreiner, Basel

1980 'The Penrose Collection of Works by Scottie Wilson', Mayor Gallery, London

1981 'The Fantastic Art of Scottie Wilson', The Scottish Gallery, Edinburgh

1986 'The Life and Work of Scottie Wilson', Third Eye Centre, Glasgow

Group exhibitions

1945 'Surrealist Diversity', Arcade Gallery, London

1947 'Exposition Internationale du Surrèalisme', Galerie Maeght, Paris

1948 '3 Types of Automatism: Ernst Martin, Paul Paun, Scottie Wilson', The London Gallery, London

1952 'Phantastiche Kunst, XX Jahrhunderts', Kunsthalle, Basel

'Tendances de la Peinture et de la Sculpture Britanniques Contemporaines', Galerie de France, Paris

1967 'Three Naïve Painters: Scottie Wilson, Margaret Baird, Gladys Hamilton Cooper', Moyan Gallery, Manchester

'International Exhibition of Naïve Painting', Circle Gallery, London

'L'Art brut; Selection de Collections de l'Art brut', Musée des Arts Décoratifs, Paris

1974 'Naïve Art in Canada', National Gallery of Canada, Ottawa

1977 'Irréguliers de l'Art', Maison de la Culture, Rennés

1978 'Les Singuliers de l'Art', Musée d'Art Moderne de la Ville de Paris

'Collection de l'Art brut', Château de Beaulieu, Lausanne

'Dada and Surrealism Revisited', Hayward Gallery, London

1979 'Britain's First International Naïve Art Exhibition', Hamilton Fine Art, London

'Outsiders', Arts Council of Great Britain, Hayward Gallery, London

'Outsiders', Louisiana Revy, Humleback, Copenhagen

'Outsiders, Konsten', Liferalchs Konsthall, Stockholm

1980 'Their Way, An Exhibition of Four Painters: Scottie Wilson, Alf O'Brian, Nicholas Evans, Ken Watts', Bede Gallery, Jarrow

'Wahn oder Wirklichkeit', Galerie Charlotte für Naive Kunst, Munich

1981 'Paris-Paris', Centre National d'Art et de Culture Georges-Pompidou

'XVI Bienal de São Paulo', São Paulo, Brazil

1982 'Two British Primitives; Alfred Wallis and Scottie Wilson', Mercury Gallery, London

'The Best of British Naïve Painters', A London Festival Exhibition at Britannic House, London
'Aftermath', The Barbican Art Gallery, London
1983 'Ascher Textiles', Redfern Gallery, London
1984 'English Contrasts', Artcurial, Paris

Public collections containing works by Scottie Wilson

United Kingdom collections

The Tate Gallery, London
The Scottish National Gallery of Modern Art, Edinburgh
Leicester Museum and Art Gallery, and other major provincial galleries

Collections outside the United Kingdom

The Museum of Modern Art, New York
The National Gallery of Canada, Ottawa
Centre National d'Art et de Culture Georges-Pompidou, Paris
Musée d'Art Moderne da la Ville de Paris
Collection de L'Art Brut, Lausanne
L'Aracine, Gagny, Paris
La Fabuloserie, Dicy, France

BIBLIOGRAPHY

Monographs

Levy, Mervyn, *Scottie Wilson*, Brook Street Gallery, London, 1966

Schreiner, Gérard A., *Scottie Wilson*, Galerie Schreiner, Basel, 1979

Thévoz, Michel, *Scottie Wilson*, Fascicules No. 4, Le Compagnie de l'Art Brut, Paris, 1965.

General books

Amory, Mark (ed.), *The Letters of Evelyn Waugh*, Weidenfeld & Nicolson, London, 1980

Barwick, F.D., *Pictures from the Douglas M. Duncan Collection*, University of Toronto Press, 1975

Cardinal, Roger, *Outsider Art*, Studio Vista, London, 1972

——*Primitive Painters*, Thames and Hudson, London, 1972

Lister, Eric and Williams, Sheldon, *Twentieth Century British Naïve and Primitive Artists*, Astagel Books, London, 1972

Lister, Eric, *Portal Painters: A Survey of British Primitive Fantasists*, Alpine Fine Arts, New York, 1982

Melly, George, *A Tribe of One: Great Naïve Painters of the British Isles*, Oxford Illustrated Press, Yeovil, 1981

Musgrave, Victor and Cardinal, Roger, *Outsiders: An Art Without Precedent in Tradition*, Arts Council of Great Britain, London, 1979

Passeron, René, *Concise Encyclopaedia of Surrealism*, Omega Books, London, 1984

Presler, G., *L'Art Brut*, Kunst Zwischen Genialitat, Cologne, 1981

Robertson, Bryan, *English Contrasts*, Artcurial, Paris, 1984

Russell Harper, J., *Naïve Art in Canada*, National Gallery of Canada, Ottawa, 1973

Thévoz, Michel and Dubuffet, Jean, *Catalogue de la Collection de l'Art Brut*, Le Compagnie de l'Art Brut, Paris, 1971

Thévoz, Michel, *L'Art Brut*, Skira, Geneva, 1975

——*Collection de l'Art brut*, Lausanne, 1976

Williams, Sheldon, *Britain's First International Naïve Art Exhibition*, Hamilton Fine Art, London, 1979

World Encyclopaedia of Naïve Art, Frederick Muller, London, 1984

Group exhibition catalogues

Dada and Surrealism Revisited, The Arts Council, London, 1978

Paris-Paris, Centre National d'Art et de Culture Georges-Pompidou, Paris, 1981

XVI Bienal de São Paulo, Volume 3; Catalogo de Arte Incomun, São Paulo, 1981

Aftermath, The Barbican Centre, London, 1982

Major articles and reviews

Agay, C., *Art Aujourd'hui*, Series No.2, November 1950, p.22

Bazarov, K., 'Outsiders', *Art & Artists*, No.13, April 1979, p.8

Blakeston, O., 'Scottie Wilson', *Arts Review*, Vol.29, Pt.4, 18 February 1977, p.106

Burland, C., 'Scottie Wilson', *Arts Review*, Vol.27, Pt.5, 7 March 1975, p.129

Burr, J., 'Scottie Wilson', *Apollo*, No.84, October 1966, p.333

Karna, E., 'Outsiders, London', *Project*, April 1979, p.131

Lambert, R.C., *Saturday Night*, Vol.50, No. 32, 17 April 1943

Laughton, Bruce, 'Scottie Wilson', *Arts Review*, Vol.20, No.11, 8 June 1968, p.331

Levy, Mervyn, 'Scottie Wilson: The Visionary Experience', *Studio*, No.172, November 1966, pp.244-247

——'Scottie Wilson's Kingdom in Kilburn', *Studio*, No.162, June 1962, pp.226-231

Mesens, E.L.T., 'Scottie Wilson', *Horizon*, Vol.XIII, No.78, June 1946

——'Scottie Wilson', *Kronick van Kunst en Kultuur*, No.11, 1 November 1946, pp.335-337

Musgrave, Victor, 'The Erotic Cosmos: Victor Musgrave Looks at the Career of Scottie Wilson', *Art & Artists*, Vol.9, Pt.7, October 1974, pp.6-9. Reprinted in *Seer*, III, June 1980, pp.22-25

Mullins, E., 'The Visionary of Kilburn', *The Weekend Telegraph*, 7 October 1964, pp.41-44

Osborne, H., 'Scottie Wilson', *Arts Review*, Vol.29, Pt.25, 9 December 1977, p.742

Russell, D., 'London: Magritte, Caro, Environments', *ARTS*, No.43, April 1969, p.50

Stahly, F., 'Scottie Wilson', *Graphis*, Vol.8, No.40, 1952, pp.124-127

Rayner, Martin, 'Outsider Art: An Introduction', *Seer*, III, June 1980, p.22
Thévoz, Michel, 'Scottie l'Analphabète', *Werk*, No.65, January-February 1978, p.86
Whittet, G.S., 'Scottie Wilson', *Studio*, 142, December 1951, pp.188-189
Winter, S.V., 'Scottie Wilson at the Artists' Market', *Artscribe*, April 1977, pp.43-44
Wykes-Joyce, M., 'Alfred Wallis and Scottie Wilson', *Arts Review*, Vol.34, Pt.11, 21 May 1982, p.263

Other articles and reviews

Daily Herald, 'Pavement Academy', 10 May 1948
Art News, No.24, December 1948, p.46
Daily Herald, 6 September 1949
Time Magazine, 19 September 1949, p.73
Apollo, No.50, October 1949, p.88
Art Digest, No.24, 15 December 1949, p.21
Werk, No.38, June 1951, p.80
Arts Canada, 'The Story Behind Our Cover', Vol.9, No.3, 1952, p.94
Schweizerische Beobochter, No.1, January 1953
Daily Telegraph and *Morning Post*, 'In Scottie Circles', 13 December 1962
The Scotsman, 'Scottie and Annie of Glasgow', 7 January 1963
Connoisseur, No.164, January 1967, p.44
Connaissance Arts, No.243, May 1972, p.27
Apollo, No.101, January 1975, p.57
L'Oeil, 'Collection de l'Art brut, Château de Beaulieu', No.270-271, January-February 1978, p.87
Verkehrszentrale, Basel, 1978, No.2, p.57

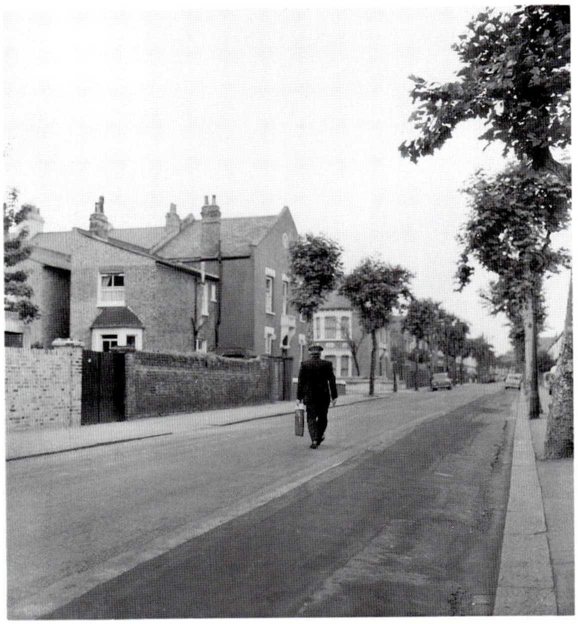

Scottie in Kilburn, *c.* 1965. Photo: Ida Kar